YOUR SPIRITUAL GIFTS

CAN HELP YOUR CHURCH GROW

C. PETER WAGNER

Regal

From Gospel Light
Ventura, California, U.S.A.

PUBLISHED BY REGAL BOOKS
FROM GOSPEL LIGHT
VENTURA, CALIFORNIA, U.S.A.

Regal PRINTED IN THE U.S.A.

Regal Books is a ministry of Gospel Light, a Christian publisher dedicated to serving the local church. We believe God's vision for Gospel Light is to provide church leaders with biblical, user-friendly materials that will help them evangelize, disciple and minister to children, youth and families.

It is our prayer that this Regal book will help you discover biblical truth for your own life and help you meet the needs of others. May God richly bless you.

For a free catalog of resources from Regal Books/Gospel Light, please call your Christian supplier or contact us at 1-800-4-GOSPEL *or* www.regalbooks.com.

Cover design by David Griffing
Interior design by Stephen Hahn

Library of Congress Cataloging-in-Publication Data
Wagner, C. Peter.
  Your spiritual gifts can help your church grow / C. Peter Wagner.—Updated and expanded ed.
    p. cm.
  Includes index.
  ISBN 0-8307-3697-2
  1. Gifts, Spiritual. 2. Church growth. I. Title.
  BT767.3.W34 2005
  234'.13—dc22   2004028920

Trade paperback ISBN 0-8307-3677-8

1 2 3 4 5 6 7 8 9 10 11 12 13 14 15 / 11 10 09 08 07 06 05

Rights for publishing this book in other languages are contracted by Gospel Light Worldwide, the international nonprofit ministry of Gospel Light. Gospel Light Worldwide also provides publishing and technical assistance to international publishers dedicated to producing Sunday School and Vacation Bible School curricula and books in the languages of the world. For additional information, visit www.gospellightworldwide.org; write to Gospel Light Worldwide, P.O. Box 3875, Ventura, CA 93006; or send an e-mail to info@gospellightworldwide.org.

Of the more than five dozen books I have written, this one clearly has helped people the most. When you read it, when you discover your spiritual gifts and when you feel the thrill of seeing others being blessed by God through your personal ministry, you will understand why!

C. Peter Wagner

CONTENTS

DIRECTORY OF THE SPIRITUAL GIFTS

In this book, 28 spiritual gifts are defined and discussed in some detail when each one comes up naturally in the general flow of the book. For easy reference, here are the gifts in the original order in which they are introduced in chapter 3, followed by the page numbers where detailed discussion of each gift begins. Consult the index for additional references to the gifts.

INTRODUCTION

We have been living in a period of history, which, if anything else, is characterized by rapid change. Many enormously significant changes have shaken the world, the Christian community and my own ministry over the 25 years since the first edition of *Your Spiritual Gifts Can Help Your Church Grow* was released. But one thing has not changed: God continues to say to the Body of Christ worldwide that the ministry of the Church must be placed in the hands of the people of God. And, in order to bring this to pass, He continues to steer the Church toward the biblical teaching on spiritual gifts as the essential foundation for the ministry of believers.

This is directly related to known principles of church growth. One thing that I have learned over a career of studying and teaching on the health and growth of the Church is that church growth carries a price tag. My friend Pastor Rick Warren of Saddleback Church, when he was teaching with me in Fuller Seminary years ago, said it as well as anyone I have heard: "For the church to grow, the pastor must give up the ministry and the people must give up the leadership." To put it another way, smaller churches will become larger ones only if the pastor does the leading and the people do the ministry. If you have had much experience in traditional churches, you will recognize this as quite a radical thought.

It is my expectation that this book will help that to happen. I can say this with considerable assurance, because feedback I have received over the past 25 years has indicated that these ideas about spiritual gifts actually work in practice. By far, I have received more sustained, positive response to this book than any of the other books I have written to date.

TWO PARADIGM SHIFTS

This book is the second revised edition of the original, not a new book. Many of the revisions reflect two "paradigm shifts" that I have experienced since the book first came out.

The first one began around 1980. This was when my friend John Wimber founded the Anaheim Vineyard Christian Fellowship and began ministering in the areas of supernatural power. I knew very little about these things, but I became intensely interested. In fact, I invited John to teach what he had been learning in my classes at Fuller Seminary. We called the course, "MC510 Signs, Wonders, and Church Growth." As Wimber taught, I found myself becoming an active participant in various power ministries. Naturally, this has influenced my views of the application of some key spiritual gifts.

My second important paradigm shift dates back to the early 1990s when I began to understand the significance of a huge international movement, which I since have come to call the New Apostolic Reformation. For the first time, I began to see that the offices of apostle and prophet were active in the Church today. Much to my surprise, around the year 2000, I realized that God had given me the gift of apostle, and other Christian leaders subsequently commissioned me into the office of apostle. In the earlier editions of this book, I did have the presence of mind to include the gift of apostle in my list of spiritual gifts, but I had no idea how to test for it on the Wagner-Modified Houts Questionnaire. In this new edition of the book, I have done two things: (1) I have revised the definition of the gift of apostle, and (2) I have added it to the questionnaire.

ONE MORE GIFT

This brings up one more change. Up to now my list included 27 spiritual gifts. However, as most readers will have observed, quite radical changes have recently come into our churches across the board in areas of worship style. I will go into more detail later on, but for now suffice it to say that I believe I have accurately discerned that there is such a thing as a spiritual gift of leading worship. So I have added it to the list, making a new total of 28 gifts.

Previous versions of the gifts inventory tested for 25 gifts, omitting apostle and martyrdom. I have not as yet come upon what I consider a decent way of testing for the gift of martyrdom, despite numerous attempts. However, I have added apostle, as I just said, and also leading worship, so the questionnaire now covers 27 of the 28 gifts.

Over the years, despite my paradigm shifts, I did not feel that I had to change any of the definitions of gifts from the time of the first edition of the book—except for the gift of apostle. I did substitute the term "deliverance" for "exorcism," primarily for semantic reasons. In the early days, I had not observed the spiritual gift of deliverance in action on a sustained basis as I do now.

Your Spiritual Gifts Can Help Your Church Grow is a much better book in this third, revised edition. If you have read the book before, I think you will enjoy it much more this time.

Chapter 1

THE REDISCOVERY OF
SPIRITUAL GIFTS

A relatively new thing happened to the Church of Jesus Christ in America around the 1970s. The third Person of the Trinity came into His own, so to speak. Yes, the Holy Spirit has always been there. Creeds, hymns and liturgies have attested to the central place of the Holy Spirit in orthodox Christian faith. Systematic theologies throughout the centuries have included sections on pneumatology, thus affirming the Holy Spirit's place in Christian thought.

But rarely, if ever, in the history of the Church has such a widespread interest in moving beyond creeds and theologies to a personal experience of the Holy Spirit in everyday life swept over the people of God to the degree that we are now seeing. One of the most prominent facets of this new experience of the Holy Spirit is the rediscovery of spiritual gifts.

FIXING THE DATE

It is fairly easy to fix the date when this new interest in the Holy Spirit began. The production of literature itself is a reasonably accurate indicator. A decent seminary library will catalog more than 50 books on the subject of spiritual gifts. Over 90 percent of

them were written after 1970. Previous to 1970, seminary gradu-
ates characteristically left their institutions knowing little or
nothing about spiritual gifts. Now, such a state of affairs would
generally be regarded as a deficiency in ministerial training.

The roots of this new thing go back to 1900, the most widely accepted date for what is now known as the classical
Pentecostal movement. During a watch night service, beginning
December 31, 1900, and ending on what was technically the first
day of the twentieth century, Charles Parham of Topeka, Kansas,
laid his hands on Agnes Ozman; she began speaking in tongues;
and the movement had begun. A fascinating chain of events led
to the famous Azusa Street Revival, which began in 1906 under
the ministry of William Seymour. And with that, the Pentecostal
movement gained high visibility and a momentum that has
never slackened.

The original intent of Pentecostal leaders was to influence
the major Christian denominations from within, reminiscent
of the early intentions of such leaders as Martin Luther and
John Wesley. But as Lutheranism was considered incompatible
with the Catholic Church in the sixteenth century and as
Methodism was considered incompatible with the Anglican
Church in the eighteenth century, so Pentecostalism was considered incompatible with the mainline American churches in
the twentieth century. Thus, as others had done before them,
Pentecostal leaders reluctantly found it necessary to establish
new denominations through which they could develop a
lifestyle directly under the influence of the Holy Spirit in an
atmosphere of freedom and mutual support. Such denominations that we know today as Assemblies of God, Pentecostal
Holiness, Church of God in Christ, Church of the Foursquare
Gospel, Church of God (Cleveland, Tennessee) and many others
were formed for that purpose.

PENTECOSTALS BECOME "RESPECTABLE"

The second phase of this movement began after World War II, when Pentecostal leaders such as Thomas Zimmerman of the Assemblies of God set out to join the mainstream. The beginnings were slow. Some of the Pentecostal denominations began to gain "respectability" by affiliating with organizations such as the National Association of Evangelicals. Thereby they helped to neutralize the opinion that Pentecostalism was a false sect to be placed alongside of Jehovah's Witnesses or Mormons or spiritists. In 1960, an Episcopal priest in Van Nuys, California, Dennis Bennett, shared with his congregation that he had experienced the Holy Spirit in the Pentecostal way, and the charismatic movement had its start. A further important movement dates to the Duquesne Weekend, named after Duquesne University, when, in 1967, the Catholic charismatics came into being.[1]

The effect of all this soon began to be felt among Christians who considered themselves neither classical Pentecostals nor charismatics. Although many of these evangelical Christians still show little interest in experiencing the "baptism in the Holy Spirit," the main distinguishing feature of these new movements is that they are appropriating the dynamic of spiritual gifts in a new and exciting way. Through their discovery of how the gifts of the Spirit are intended to operate in the Body of Christ, the Holy Spirit is now being transformed from abstract doctrine to dynamic experience.

HOW "NEW" IS THE "NEW THING"?

If my research into the part spiritual gifts have played throughout church history is any indication, the general picture of spiritual gifts is one of ambiguity. Those who are trying to make a point one way or another by historical references are generally able to do so. Some who are cool on spiritual gifts, for example, say that many of the gifts went out of use in the churches after the age of the apostles. The intellectual center of this effort is at Dallas Theological Seminary, an interdenominational school that has looked with disfavor on the Pentecostal/charismatic movement of recent decades.

John Walvoord, former president of Dallas Seminary, feels that miracles have declined in the Church since the age of the apostles.[2] His colleague Merrill Unger writes that the fact that "miraculous charismata passed away after the apostolic period is well attested by church history." Unger argues that the miraculous gifts were given basically as credentials to the apostles for confirmation of the gospel, and therefore they passed away "when apostles no longer existed and the Christian faith no longer needed such outward signs to confirm it."[3]

CESSATIONISM

Merrill Unger makes reference to Benjamin B. Warfield of Princeton Seminary, who, back in 1918, wrote a book called *Counterfeit Miracles*, later published under the title *Miracles: Yesterday and Today, True and False*. Other than the *Scofield Reference Bible*, it has been the most influential book written in America against the validity of the charismatic gifts today. Warfield argues, "These gifts were . . . distinctively the authentication of the Apostles. . . . Their function thus confined them to distinctively the Apostolic Church, and they necessarily passed away with it."[4] As we will discuss in more detail later on, this point of view, called cessationism, continues to be strongly argued on dogmatic grounds by a certain circle of evangelical leaders in America today.

One of the reasons that this theory of discontinuity of some of the gifts has gained a degree of support is that not much evidence to the contrary has been gleaned from history. Scholars more favorable to spiritual gifts, in fact, had not aggressively challenged Warfield on his own intellectual level.

In part, until recently, scholarly contributions from Pentecostals had not been forthcoming, because the early Pentecostals had developed a strong anti-intellectualism. Ministers who set themselves in opposition to the Pentecostals and who relegated them to false cults were usually seminary trained. On the other hand, Pentecostals had recruited most of their ministers from the ranks of the working class on the basis of proven exercise of spiritual gifts and not because they had attained academic degrees. They often looked upon seminaries with a degree of suspicion.

For years, a kind of cold war existed between the Pentecostals and the seminaries. But now this, for good or for bad, has largely been resolved. Several Pentecostal denominations now have accredited seminaries. I say "for good or for bad," because accredited seminaries are not by any means an unqualified blessing. Although they undoubtedly can help provide scholarship for their movements, they at the same time may contribute to the process of "redemption and lift," which has been known to separate churches from the working class from which they emerged. The history of the Methodist movement is example enough of how this can and does happen.

Nevertheless, Pentecostal scholars are already digging more deeply into historical records to find precedents for their emphases. Pentecostal scholars have organized the Society for Pentecostal Studies. And in 1993, Jack Deere, who taught cessationism at Dallas Theological Seminary, wrote *Surprised by the Power of the Spirit*, which many people consider the definitive refutation of Warfield's and Dallas's cessationist doctrine.

WHAT HISTORY TELLS US

In the second century, both Justin Martyr and Irenaeus acknowledged that the miraculous gifts were in operation in the Church. In the third century, Hippolytus made reference to one of his own writings, "On Charismatic Gifts," although the essay itself has never been located. In the same century, Tertullian observed with approval the exercise of spiritual gifts, and then himself converted to Montanism, a kind of third-century charismatic movement, eventually declared heretical by many of the mainline Christians of the day. Bishop Hilary of the fourth century spoke of the exercise of the gifts with favor, as did John Chrysostom. The great theologian of the fifth century, Augustine, is interpreted as supporting both those who say the gifts blinked off and those who say they continued. However, James Gordon King, Jr., has discovered that Augustine "completely reversed his views on miracles. Originally he disputed their continuance into his day. He later taught their present validity and claimed to be an eyewitness to some miracles."[5]

Thomas Aquinas, in the thirteenth century, considered the charismatic gifts essential to the Church, although he did not address the matter of whether they actually had continued after the First Apostolic Age.[6] Other references to spiritual gifts between Augustine and the time of the Reformation—a span of more than 1,000 years—are sparse, but undoubtedly much gold is yet to be mined by scholars who will pursue the field. It is reasonably certain that evidence will continue to build showing that charismatic gifts were, in fact, operative in segments of the Church throughout many different eras of church history.

THE REFORMERS

The two most prominent theologians at the time of the Protestant Reformation, Martin Luther and John Calvin, had little to say about spiritual gifts. Although Luther did not restrict the possibility of the use of the miraculous gifts to the Apostolic Age, neither did he expect them to be manifested in his churches. Calvin is generally interpreted as contending that the gifts had ceased with the Apostolic Age, although he also seemed to be open to the idea that they could have surfaced later on. In fact, he once included Luther among modern "apostles."[7]

The most extensive treatment of the work of the Holy Spirit between the Reformation and the twentieth century comes from the pen of John Owen of seventeenth-century England. His writings were influential in the thought of the later Reformed or Calvinistic theologians. Owen does recognize that gifts are valid in the Church, but he may have been the first to distinguish between extraordinary gifts and ordinary gifts, a distinction common in later Reformed theology. Extraordinary gifts, supposedly restricted to the days of the apostles, include tongues, miracles, healings and the offices of apostle, prophet and evangelist. Similar thinking appears in people such as Abraham Kuyper in the nineteenth century and Benjamin Warfield in the twentieth century.

John Wesley, the father of Methodism and the subsequent holiness movements, is in a way the stepfather of the Pentecostal movement. His openness to the Scriptures and the New Testament pattern, as well as his stress on the responsibility of the individual Christian, helped set the stage. But, although he mentioned spiritual gifts on occasion, he was "unsystematic and incomplete in his treatment of the gifts."[8] He was so inconsistent that his direct contribution to subsequent understanding of spiritual gifts must be considered minimal.

Throughout church history, marginal groups came into being that were characterized by, among other things, the use of spiritual gifts. Many of these groups were considered fanatical and even heretical by mainstream Christians of their day. One wonders whether such criticism might not have been parallel to mainstream Christian ridicule and persecution of the Pentecostals in the early part of the twentieth century. Groups such as the Waldenses, the Albigenses, the Camisards, the Jansenists, the early Quakers, the Shakers and the Irvingites have been mentioned as using the charismatic gifts. Many of them, predictably, suffered persecution at the hands of other Christians who had not come to terms with the operation of spiritual gifts in their midst.

When I say that a new thing happened around the 1970s, I mean just that. Although charismatic gifts may have been manifested in some segments of the Body of Christ throughout Christian history, nevertheless, today in America and in other parts of the world their use is far more widespread. The recognition of spiritual gifts crosses the boundaries of more ecclesiastical traditions than in any other time this side of the first century.

THE MINISTRY OF ALL BELIEVERS

Martin Luther permanently changed Christendom when, among other things, he rediscovered the *priesthood* of all believers. Still, Lutheranism, along with Calvinism, retained much of the clericalism of the Roman Catholic Church. One wonders why it took more than 400 years for the churches born of the Protestant Reformation to rediscover the biblical teaching of the *ministry* of all believers.

I believe that 1972 can be considered the date that the concept of the ministry of all believers attained a permanent status in contemporary Christianity. In 1972, Ray Stedman's book *Body Life* was published, and it became a best-seller. In his book, this highly respected non-Pentecostal leader argued that spiritual gifts were *okay* in the Body of Christ. Although his list of the gifts was shorter than some others (because he also happened to be a cessationist), he showed how spiritual gifts, the ministry of all believers and "Body life" had brought health, vitality and excitement to his dynamic Peninsula Bible Church in Palo Alto, California.

The ripple effects of the publication of *Body Life* have had such a profound influence that rare is the church today that advocates that the professional pastor or staff should do all the

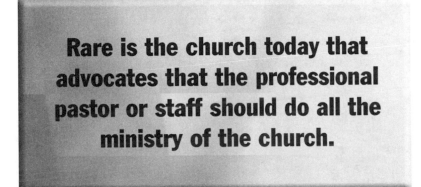

Rare is the church today that advocates that the professional pastor or staff should do all the ministry of the church.

ministry of the church. Although some churches may have not been able to implement it as rapidly as others, most affirm at least in theory that laypeople should be empowered to discover their spiritual gifts and through them participate in the authentic ministry of the church.

How this can become a reality in any church, as well as in the workplace, is what this book is all about.

REFLECTIONS

1. Suppose we agree that the Bible clearly teaches that all believers have at least one spiritual gift for ministry. How, then, can you explain why churches

throughout the centuries did not include this in their central teaching?

2. Why would it be that many Pentecostal leaders in the first part of our century began preaching on spiritual gifts but did not teach that the ministry of the church should be done mostly by laypeople?

3. Do you personally know any believers who feel that some of the spiritual gifts mentioned in the Bible went out of use after the first century? What do you think of this?

4. Discuss the difference between Martin Luther's doctrine of the priesthood of all believers and Peter Wagner's doctrine of the ministry of all believers.

5. After reading about some of the history of the practice of spiritual gifts, where would you say your own church fits?

Notes

1. For a concise summary of the major details of the historical development of these "three streams," see Charles E. Hummel, *Fire in the Fireplace: Contemporary Charismatic Renewal* (Downers Grove, IL: InterVarsity Press, 1978).
2. John F. Walvoord, *The Holy Spirit* (Grand Rapids, MI: Zondervan Publishing Company, 1954), pp. 173-187.
3. Merrill F. Unger, *The Baptism and Gifts of the Holy Spirit* (Chicago: Moody Press, 1974), p. 139.
4. Benjamin B. Warfield, *Miracles: Yesterday and Today, True and False* (Grand Rapids, MI: Eerdmans Publishing Company, 1953), p. 6.
5. James Gordon King Jr., "A Brief Overview of Historical Beliefs in Gifts of the Spirit" (unpublished paper, 1977). This paper is a compilation of preliminary notes in preparation for a Ph.D. dissertation at New York University. A good bit of the historical information in this section is gleaned from King's paper. Hummel's book, *Fire in the Fireplace*, also has a helpful discussion of historical evidence for the gifts (see pp. 164-168).
6. Theodore Jungkuntz, "Secularization Theology, Charismatic Renewal,

and Luther's Theology of the Cross," *Concordia Theological Monthly* (January 1971), p. 72.

7. King, "A Brief Overview of Historical Beliefs in Gifts of the Spirit," p. 8.

8. Ibid., p. 14.

Chapter 2

IGNORANCE IS NOT BLISS

Who needs to know about spiritual gifts?

You need to know about spiritual gifts if

1. you are a Christian believer;
2. you believe that Jesus is your Lord and you want to love Him, please Him and follow Him in the best way possible; and
3. you want your church to be a healthy, attractive, growing group of people showing forth God's love in your community.

"I do not want you to be ignorant [of spiritual gifts]" are the inspired words of the apostle Paul in 1 Corinthians 12:1. The church in Corinth, to which Paul was writing, desperately needed instruction on spiritual gifts. But today, countless other churches in Philadelphia, San Antonio, Kansas City, Seattle, Nashville and your city as well, also need to know about spiritual gifts. Despite a widespread renewal of interest in the Holy Spirit and His ministry in our day, church after church in America and in other parts of the world still remain ignorant of this tremendous God-given dynamic for church vitality and growth just waiting to be released.

Such ignorance is by no means bliss!

I am convinced that ignorance of spiritual gifts may be a chief cause of retarded church growth today. It also may be at the root of much of the discouragement, insecurity, frustration and guilt that plague many Christians and curtail their total effectiveness for God.

GEORGE BARNA'S WAKE-UP CALL

Ignorance of spiritual gifts might be seen as a relatively trivial matter if the current trend were toward a better understanding of the gifts in our churches across the board. Such, however, does not appear to be the case. One of our most respected church researchers, George Barna, did a study of Christians and their spiritual gifts over a five-year period. His research shows that the trend is, in fact, just the opposite. In 1995 Barna found that only 4 percent of born-again adults in America did not believe that God had given them a spiritual gift (not a bad percentage, in my opinion). However, by 2000 the figure had gone up to 21 percent, five times the number![1] I would hope that the percentage in your church is better than that. I hope that by the time you finish this book and apply the biblical teachings to your congregation, 100 percent of your members will know that they have a spiritual gift (or gifts) and that most of them can identify their gift (or gifts) by name.

YOUR MOST BASIC STEP

Are you really the person God wants you to be? Are you fulfilling all of God's destiny for your life? If not, I'm sure that the Holy Spirit wants to head you in a different and more productive direction.

Be assured that simply dispelling the fog of ignorance about spiritual gifts is no magic formula for instant spirituality. Your discipleship is a tender and complex combination of factors, which constantly need to be evaluated and reevaluated. Other things being equal, however, you may soon come to experience a liberating, invigorating and uplifting encounter with God's Holy Spirit as you discover what I consider to be the most basic step that you as a Christian need to take in order to define God's will for your life—knowing your spiritual gift.

To many, this could sound so radical that they might begin to doubt my credibility. They may wonder if perhaps I have not overstated myself.

I do not think I have. I personally feel strongly that what I have said is valid. The vitality that coming to terms with spiritual gifts contributes to Christian discipleship has been impressed on me from two sources. The first source is the Word of God:

> All Scripture is given by inspiration of God . . . that the man of God may be . . . thoroughly equipped for every good work (2 Tim. 3:16-17).

The first source for a sense of direction in finding ourselves spiritually, then, must be the Bible, and there is no substitute for it.

The other source, although secondary, has been equally essential for my conclusion—my own experience. On a recent radio interview, I was asked what was my most important spiritual experience other than my conversion. I did not hesitate in answering that it was discovering my spiritual gifts. As this book progresses, I will describe in some detail how this happened in my personal life, so I will not stop to elaborate here.

Let's go directly to the primary source, then—the Word of God.

GOD'S WAY FOR FINDING GOD'S WILL

One of the Scripture texts most frequently recommended to new Christians for memory is Romans 12:1-2. It certainly was among those I first memorized when I became a Christian more than 50 years ago, and I have never forgotten it:

> I beseech you therefore, brethren, by the mercies of God, that you present your bodies a living sacrifice, holy, acceptable to God, which is your reasonable service. And do not be conformed to this world, but be transformed by the renewing of your mind, that you may prove what is that good and acceptable and perfect will of God.

The last phrase of this passage is the one that makes it so appealing to new Christians. Doing the "good and acceptable and perfect will of God" is the sincere, heartfelt desire of virtually every person who has been truly born again. When we realize that Jesus paid the ultimate price—His blood poured out on the cross—to save us, the first thing we usually say is, "Thank You, God. I love You for what You did. I want to please You. I want to serve You. Now please tell me what You want me to do."

These two verses from Romans, however, pose a problem to veteran Christians, to say nothing of new ones. To be honest, they are not very practical.

By pure coincidence, the week I was first researching the meaning of this text, my pastor at the time preached a sermon on the same passage. Because I knew I was going to be writing on it that week, I listened with a great deal of attention. I was impressed with his unusual combination of exegetical and homiletical energy that he seemed to be exerting in order to try to make the meaning clear to the congregation. The meaning of such concepts as presenting bodies a living sacrifice or not being conformed to this world or being transformed by the renewing of your mind is far from self-evident to an average reader. They are wonderful verses, but rather abstract to say the least. I left church that morning still a bit unclear as to how all this applied to me personally.

As I reflected back on my own spiritual pilgrimage, I could recall that these verses I had memorized in the early days undoubtedly did something for my life, but not very much. They felt good to recite, for one thing. For another, they reminded me that part of living the kind of life that would please God was to consecrate myself to Him. But where they let me down was in the practical area of actually finding God's will. Yes, I wanted to do the "good and acceptable and perfect will of God," but all I could deduce from Romans 12:1-2 was that the more consecrated I became, the more clearly I would then be able to know the will of God.

Consecration Theology

This idea, which I now call consecration theology, was fairly widespread among the circle of Christian friends with whom I was moving in those days. One of the major symbols of improved consecration among the believers I knew was the famous Keswick Christian Campground in New Jersey, near where I lived at the time. When critical decisions came up in life, we were frequently advised to spend a few days at Keswick. There, we were assured, we would enter into the "victorious life," and through it God's will for us would become clear. As I look back, I see that God, by His grace, did give me certain guidance through consecration theology. However, I had a lingering feeling that there must be some better way of finding God's pathway for the future.

A consecrated Christian life is certainly necessary for doing God's will. Nothing I say should be taken either to deny or to dilute that fact. But in order to understand the truly *practical* methodology for finding the "good and acceptable and perfect will of God," we need to read forward to Romans 12:3-6, not backward to Romans 12:1-2. This is the better way. This is digging a foundation by using a Caterpillar tractor rather than a teaspoon.

Gift Theology

The key to coming to practical terms with the will of God for our lives is "to think soberly" of ourselves, according to Romans 12:3. This means that each of us needs a realistic self-evaluation as a starting point. The *Phillips* translation says, "Try to have a sane estimate of your capabilities."

Two steps need to be taken to arrive at this realistic self-evaluation, one negative and one positive.

Negatively, we are not allowed to think more highly of ourselves than we ought to think. In evaluating ourselves, therefore, there is no room for pride. Sober judgments always assume humility. If we must err, it is better to err on the side of being too humble rather than being too proud. But neither extreme is necessary in light of the way God has arranged things for His children.

Positively, we are to recognize that part of our spiritual constitution is a "measure of faith" (v. 3), which God has distributed to every Christian person. The implication is that every Christian may receive a different measure, and thereby every Christian is unique. But unique in what sense? Before Paul answers this question, he gives us the analogy that he uses extensively to explain spiritual gifts, namely, the analogy of the human body.

From Romans 12:4, we learn that a simple overview of our own physical body will give us what we might term a hermeneutical key to unlock the biblical teaching on spiritual gifts. Hermeneutics is simply the theological word for biblical interpretation. So in order to comprehend the biblical teaching on spiritual gifts, we do well to keep a mental picture of our human body before us at all times.

The Hermeneutical Key

This hermeneutical key is surprisingly uncomplicated. It does not involve knowledge of advanced anatomy or physiology or biological science. It simply requires the recognition that our one physical body is made up of many members, and that each member of the one body has a different function. In other words, if we understand that we cannot pick up anything with our ear and that we cannot hear with our hand, we have the clue we need. Bodily members are designed to do their specific thing and no more. We err if we expect them to do what they are not designed to do. But whatever they do benefits the whole body.

With that, Paul goes on to say in Romans 12:5 that the Body of Christ operates exactly like the human body. Each Christian is a member of the Body of Christ, and as such has a particular function to perform just as the ear or the hand does. Furthermore, all are members of the same Body, so in a very real sense all believers need each other.

That leads us to more questions. If I am a member of the Body, how do I know whether I am an ear or a hand or some other member? How do I know how God wants me to function?

The answer: Your purpose in the Body is determined by your spiritual gift or combination of gifts. After Paul says that we are members one of another, he adds, "Having then *gifts* differing according to the grace that is given to us" (v. 6),[2] and then he begins a list of specific gifts.

My conclusion from this passage of Scripture, then, is that gift theology is clearly more helpful for knowing God's will for your life in a practical way than is consecration theology. To do the "good and acceptable and perfect will of God" you must think soberly of yourself. To think soberly, you must be realistic

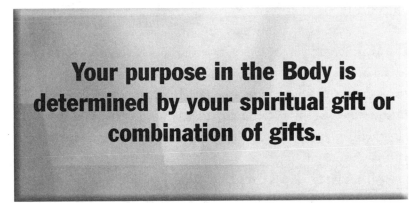

Your purpose in the Body is determined by your spiritual gift or combination of gifts.

about your measure of faith. Your measure of faith is the spiritual gift that has determined which member of the Body God has designed you to be, and it therefore reveals to you the special task God has given you to perform, presumably for the rest of your life.

WHAT IS THE BODY OF CHRIST?

What, precisely, is the Body of Christ, to which we have been introduced? Because the Bible says that we Christians are all one Body in Christ, we understand that it is a group of believers. In other biblical passages, the Body is explicitly equated with the Church. Ephesians 1, for example, talks about God's setting Christ above all principality and power, putting all things under His feet and giving Him "to be head over all things to the *church, which is His body*" (vv. 22-23). Colossians 1 says practically the same thing, namely that Jesus "is the head of *the body, the church*" (v. 18). So when I use "Body of Christ" in this book, I mean the same thing that the Bible means, namely the Christian Church.

The Church, of course, exists at many levels. It is the local fellowship of believers; it is the national denomination; it is the mission agency; and it is also the universal group of people from all countries of the world who acknowledge Christ as Lord and strive to serve Him. The Body of Christ refers to all of these.

More broadly even, the Church, namely the people of God, exists in a real way in the workplace six days a week as well as in the congregational groups that gather on Sundays. What you do in the workplace is a legitimate form of ministry, and that ministry will be ever so much more effective if it revolves around your spiritual gift.

Although I will use the term "Body of Christ" occasionally to refer to the universal Church, I will use it mostly to refer to the local congregation of believers because it is there that the majority of believers discover, develop and use their spiritual gifts in an organized way.

God Himself, of course, is the One who designed the Body of Christ. Therefore, before we ask how *we* should organize it, we need to ask how *He* has organized it.

How the Body of Christ Is Organized

On the one hand, God did not plan that the Body of Christ should be organized around the model of a dictatorship where just one person rules, benevolent as that person might be. On the other hand, neither did God intend that it should be a democracy where every member rules. This latter point needs to be emphasized, especially here in America where our civil culture prides itself so much on democracy, and where this frequently is carried over into the churches.

During my 25 years as an ordained Congregational minister, I slowly came to the reluctant conclusion that for growing churches a strict congregational form of government can be like a millstone around their neck. A democratic form of government is reasonably functional for churches of 100 or 200 members, but when churches pass the 200 mark and reach 500 or 1,000 or more, they often will find their growth stalled unless their administrative system is streamlined. Check it out. Few megachurches in this day and age function with a congregational government. They have discovered that making decisions in large, congregationally governed churches is like trying to turn the Queen Mary with an oar! It is unnecessarily difficult and energy consuming.

Instead of a dictatorship or a democracy, then, God has chosen to make the Body of Christ an *organism*, Jesus being the head and each member functioning with one or more spiritual gifts. Understanding spiritual gifts becomes the foundational key to understanding the organization of the Church.

For years I watched Grace Community Church in Sun Valley, California, sustain an incredible growth rate, reaching a current weekend attendance of almost 8,000 people. One of its strengths was being intentionally structured around the concept of spiritual gifts. Pastor John MacArthur says, "No local congregation will be what it should be, what Jesus prayed that it would be, what the Holy Spirit gifted it and empowered it to be, until it understands spiritual gifts."[3] John MacArthur is right, not only because he has proved that it works, but because he has also captured the biblical concept of the organization of the Body.

The major biblical passages on spiritual gifts reinforce the above conclusion. It cannot be mere coincidence that in all three of the most explicit passages on spiritual gifts—Romans 12, 1 Corinthians 12 and Ephesians 4—the gifts are explained in the context of the Body. "God has set the members, each one of them, in the body just as He pleased" (1 Cor. 12:18). This means not only that God has designed the Body on the model of an organism but that He has also gone so far as to determine what the function of each of the individual members should be. Therefore, if you decide to organize your church around spiritual gifts, you are simply uncovering what God has already willed for your particular segment of Christ's Body.

WHO HAS A SPIRITUAL GIFT?

Not everybody has a spiritual gift. Unbelievers, for example, do not. But every Christian person who is committed to Jesus and truly a member of His Body has at least one gift, or quite possibly more. The Bible says that every Christian has received a gift (see 1 Pet. 4:10), and that "the manifestation of the Spirit is given to each one for the profit of all" (1 Cor. 12:7). First Corinthians 12:18 stresses that *every one* of the members is placed in the Body according to God's design. Possessing a spiritual gift is an important part of the makeup of every Christian.

This comes as good news to the average believer. It is pleasant to be reminded that God knows me, He loves me and He considers me special enough to give me a personal gift so that I can serve Him. It is especially true in a society such as ours in America where many school districts establish special programs for "gifted children." The implication is that ordinary citizens are not gifted, just a few of them are. Not so in the Body of Christ! God gifts us all.

Gift-Mixes

Many Christians are multigifted. I would suspect that probably the majority of Christians, or perhaps even all, have what we could call a gift-mix, instead of just a single gift.

Given the variety of spiritual gifts, the degrees of giftedness in each personal case and the multiple ministries through which each gift can be exercised, the particular combination of these qualities that I have been given and the combination that you have been given may be the most important factor in determining our spiritual personalities. We are used to the idea that each person has his or her own personality. My wife, Doris, and I have three daughters, all born of the same parents and raised in the same household, but they are each unique. God's children are probably similar. All Christians are unique members of the Body of Christ, and their individual identity is determined to a significant degree by the gift-mix they have been given.

The health of the Church and its subsequent growth depend on this fact. Nazarene scholar, W. T. Purkiser, asserts that "every true function of the body of Christ has a 'member' to perform it, and every member has a function to perform."[4] I realize that it comes as a surprise to some Christians, who have been only marginally active in church for years, to find out that they are needed, wanted and gifted to do their part in their local church, to say nothing of their role in the workplace. But it is true. There is no substitute for finding your gift-mix and knowing for sure that you are supernaturally equipped to do just what God has designed you to do.

Women Are Equally Gifted

I wish that I did not have to point out this out, but, unfortunately, I do. Paul says that the Spirit has distributed the gifts "to each one for the profit of all" (1 Cor. 12:7). Most people agree that "each one" includes both women and men. Unfortunately, the *King James Version* says "to every man" and some still insist that it should be taken literally. It should not. Women, as well as men, are members of the Body and they receive all the spiritual gifts.

I felt badly some time ago when I read an article by Nancy Hardesty in which she argues, with a good bit of verve, that women have spiritual gifts, too. As I read, I felt badly, not because of the article itself, which was excellent, but because such an article had to be written at all. In the article, Hardesty laments that women have been assigned a disproportionately low profile by evangelical churches in general. Yes, we have made considerable progress since then, but I feel that I still must make the point.

If women, who constitute more than 50 percent of the church membership, would be encouraged and allowed to use their spiritual gifts on all levels, a tremendous dynamic for growth would be released. Nancy Hardesty also points out another item that might even be more important: "Ultimately the refusal to allow women to fully use their gifts in the church and in the world is a form of blasphemy against the Holy Spirit."[5] These are strong words, but when we think it through theologically, most will agree that she has a good point.

GOD'S GIFTS AND GOD'S CALL

Christians often speak of their "calling." Part of our religious vocabulary is that "God has *called* me to do such and such" or "I don't believe God is *calling* me to do such and such." It is helpful to recognize that a person's call and his or her spiritual gift are closely associated.

When related to the objective of doing God's will or functioning in the Body of Christ, a person's *general* call should be seen as equivalent to his or her spiritual gift. No better framework exists within which to interpret a person's call than a specific gift-mix. God does not give a gift that He does not *call* the recipient to use, nor does He *call* someone to do something for Him without equipping that person with the necessary gift or gifts to do it.

Besides the *general* calling, however, a person will also have a *specific* calling. Some like to refer to this specific call as one's "ministry." So the ministry or the specific call determines the particular way or the particular setting in which God wishes you to exercise the gift or gifts He has given you. For example, some might have the gift of teaching and be called specifically to use that gift among children; while others might use the gift of teaching on the radio or in writing books or in the pulpit. Some might have the missionary gift and be called to use that gift in Zambia; while others might be called to Paraguay or to Sri Lanka or to a different ethnic group in their own American city. Within the general calling provided by each gift, then, there are many specific callings in which such a gift is to be ministered.

WHAT IS A SPIRITUAL GIFT?

At this point, we need to pause and define just what "spiritual gift" means. The working definition I will use is as follows:

> *A spiritual gift is a special attribute given by the Holy Spirit to every member of the Body of Christ, according to God's grace, for use within the context of the Body.*

This is as tight and economical a definition as I have been

able to formulate and still retain what I consider to be the essential elements. Several of these elements—namely "special attribute," "given by the Holy Spirit" and "to every member of the Body of Christ"—have been sufficiently discussed. Two phrases remain.

Charisma

"According to God's grace" is a phrase that moves us into the biblical words themselves. The common Greek word for "spiritual gift" is *charisma;* the plural is *charismata.* It becomes immediately obvious that our contemporary terms "charismatic movement" or "charismatics" are derived from this Greek word. But note something else. "Charisma" comes from the root word *charis,* which in Greek means "grace." A close relationship exists, then, between spiritual gifts and the grace of God.

Although a thorough biblical word study may not be called for here, I think it would be helpful to note a couple of things concerning the Greek words.

First, "charisma" and "charismata" do not only mean "spiritual gifts." They are used with other meanings in the Bible such as in Romans 6:23: "For the wages of sin is death, but the gift [charisma] of God is eternal life in Christ Jesus our Lord."

Second, "charismata" is not the only word used in the New Testament for spiritual gifts, although it is the most common one. For example, in 1 Corinthians 12:1, "Now concerning spiritual gifts, brethren," the Greek word *pneumatikos,* more literally "spiritual things" or "spirituals," is used. As this theme is elaborated in the rest of the same chapter, however, "charismata" is subsequently used five times. Another word used for spiritual gifts is *domata* (singular, *doma*) found in Ephesians 4:8. "Domata" is a more general Greek word for "gifts." But here in the context it is also closely related to "grace" in the preceding verse: "But to each one of us grace [charis] was given according to the measure of Christ's gift" (Eph. 4:7). This phrase is reminiscent of the "measure of faith" of Romans 12:3, which also is tied in to "charismata" in Romans 12:6.

The major purpose in discussing this is to indicate the intimate relationship that spiritual gifts have to the grace of God. This explains why I include "according to God's grace" in the working definition of "spiritual gift."

The Context of the Body

The final phrase in the definition is "for use within the context of the Body." Wherever the church is found, it must function according to God's design. His design is for every member to minister with his or her spiritual gift on a regular basis.

Where, then, is the Church found? The root meaning of the biblical word for Church, *ekklesia,* is "the people of God." Sometimes, such as on Sundays, the people of God are gathered in their congregations, but during the week they are mostly scattered throughout the workplace. The terminology I like best for this is "nuclear Church" (believers as they meet in congregations) and "extended Church" (believers as they are in the workplace). It stands to reason that wherever the people of God are at the moment, their spiritual gifts should be available for ministry.

The idea of ministry in the extended Church is relatively new. It has only been gaining widespread acceptance since about 1997 or 1998. I did not mention it in the previous two editions of this book. Because it is new, the specific ways that spiritual gifts are to be used for ministry in the workplace are still being developed. Furthermore, the leadership of the extended Church is not yet as well defined as the leadership of the nuclear Church, and it takes leadership to make sure that the members of the Body are in their proper place and that proper doors are opened for them to use their spiritual gifts.

I say this to explain why most of the examples of using spiritual gifts in this book lean more toward ministry by the nuclear Church than by the extended Church. I would hope that one of these days either I or someone else will have enough material to do a book specifically on how spiritual gifts are used by believers of the extended Church, the workplace.

Meanwhile, when I say that gifts should be used in "the context of the Body," I do not mean that gifts are always inward looking, for use only within the Church and for the mutual benefit of Christians. Many gifts, such as evangelist, missionary and service, are designed to benefit those who are not yet members of the Body. Whenever and wherever the Church is to minister, both inwardly and outwardly, the ministry is best done through gifted believers.

DISCOVER, DEVELOP AND USE YOUR GIFT

If spiritual gifts, functioning as they should, are as important to God, to the Church and to individual Christians as I have tried to describe, something better be done about them in a practical, personal way. This is not just a theory; it is practice.

In light of the clear teaching of God's Word, I do not think I am overstating it when I say that one of the primary spiritual exercises for any Christian person is to discover, develop and use his or her spiritual gift. Other spiritual exercises may be equally as important: worship, prayer, reading God's Word, feeding the hungry, the sacraments or what have you. But I do not know of anything *more* important than discovering, developing and using spiritual gifts.

Believers desiring to do the will of God, but who do not know exactly how they are intended to function in the Body of Christ, need to give top priority to discovering gifts. Elizabeth O'Connor, from the Church of the Savior in Washington, D.C., a church nationally known for the use of spiritual gifts, puts it this way: "We ask to know the will of God without guessing that his will is written into our very beings. We perceive that will when we discern our gifts."[6]

"Discover" comes before "develop" in the sequence, because spiritual gifts are received, not achieved. God gives the gifts at His own discretion. First Corinthians 12:11 talks about the Spirit distributing gifts "to each one individually *as He wills*." Later in verse 18, the text says that God sets the members in the Body "just *as He pleased*." God has not entrusted any human being to give spiritual gifts. No pastor, no district superintendent, no seminary president, not even the Pope himself is qualified to distribute spiritual gifts.

Furthermore, no one works real hard and is then rewarded with a gift. They are gifts of grace and, as such, they emerge from God with no reference to the degree of merit or sanctification that the recipient may have attained. The fact that they are given to brand-new Christians before they have had time to mature spiritually confirms this.

IS "DISCOVERING GIFTS" COUNTERPRODUCTIVE?

Gene Getz, one of America's outstanding Bible teachers and church leaders, disagrees with the idea that it is important to Christians to discover their spiritual gifts. For many years, he himself taught that Christians should make an effort to discover gifts, but later he reversed his position.[7]

Getz's point of view deserves thoughtful consideration. For one thing, he is a thorough Bible student and he would not be inclined to draw such conclusions hastily. For another, and directly apropos to this book, the church he planted back in the 1970s, Fellowship Bible Church, enjoyed remarkable growth. In articulating the philosophy of ministry for his church, Getz stresses the concept of "body maturity." He emphasizes faith, hope and love along with the leadership qualities listed in 1 Timothy 3 and Titus 1 instead of emphasizing spiritual gifts.

In his book *Building Up One Another*, Getz lists the reasons he rejects the idea of discovering spiritual gifts. These reasons serve to catalog some of the pitfalls we need to avoid, no matter which position we decide to take. It would be well to mention them here so that we can keep them in mind as we move along with the discussion. Let me summarize them:

1. *Confusion.* Teaching Christians to discover spiritual gifts they received at conversion has, in fact, caused many people, even mature believers, to become confused.
2. *Rationalization.* Some tend to fix their attention on a supposed gift and use it as a rationalization for not fulfilling other biblical responsibilities. For example, some might say they have the gift of pastoring, but not of teaching. Or others might say that they do not have the gift of evangelism because they feel uncomfortable sharing Christ.
3. *Self-deception.* Some people think they have a spiritual gift when they really don't.

Getz is strong on this teaching because, as he says, "it suddenly dawned on me one day" that nowhere in 1 Corinthians 12, Romans 12 or Ephesians 4 "can we find any exhortation for individual Christians to 'look for' or to 'try to discover' their spiritual gift or gifts."[8]

I have considered Getz's position quite carefully. Questions about it often come up in my seminars. I hesitate to contradict him because, after all, he is a successful church planter and has seen vigorous church growth under his ministry.

Nevertheless, I will say that I do not believe Getz has given sufficient consideration to Romans 12:1-6. I do not have to go into detail, because I explained it earlier in this chapter, except to point out once again what seems to me to be a clear biblical relationship between having a gift (see v. 6), thinking soberly of oneself (see v. 3) and doing the "good and acceptable and perfect will of God" (v. 2).

GOD'S PLAN A IS BEST

Now I will be the first to admit that there are many mature, faithful and useful Christian people who are doing God's will without being able to describe in clear terms what their specific gifts might be. Certainly many believers through the centuries, throughout the world and specifically here in America—previous to the "new thing" I spoke about in chapter 1—have been doing God's will in outstanding ways. Many are in fact using their spiritual gifts without being able to articulate what they are doing. Nevertheless, I sincerely believe such believers are operating under God's "Plan B." I think Romans 12:1-6 is clear enough to teach us that God's "Plan A" is for members of the Body of Christ to be conscious of the part each one plays in "the whole body, joined and knit together" (Eph. 4:16). Plan B may be functional, but in my opinion Plan A is God's best.

The fact that many churches whose philosophy of ministry is Plan B are growing, reaffirms what church growth leaders often state: Church growth is complex. It is possible for a church to score low on one growth principle and still grow if other growth principles happen to be operating effectively. A particular view on spiritual gifts is not some surefire formula for church growth. But in *many cases* (not all) an awakening to spiritual gifts, mobilizing the membership around the gifts as biblically identified and defined, and encouraging the Body to begin functioning with its members working together by the power of the Holy Spirit will help a church get out of the growth doldrums as surely as a vaccination will prevent smallpox.

The objections Gene Getz raises to the practical discovery and use of spiritual gifts are real. Confusion, rationalization and self-deception can and do pose serious problems. But they are not insuperable obstacles. Confusion can be eliminated when strong biblical teaching on gifts is provided in a context of sensitive pastoral care. Rationalization is less useful as a cop-out when the proper relationship between gifts and roles is clarified, which I will explain in considerable detail later on. Self-deception evaporates when the Body functions well enough so that members share their perceptions of each other's gifts with openness and love.

Clearing Away Some Problems

Before finishing the subject of discovering spiritual gifts, we need to look briefly at two sets of texts that have caused problems for some people.

The first text is a pair of related verses, 1 Corinthians 12:31 and 1 Corinthians 14:1. Both of them say to "desire" or "covet" spiritual gifts. At first glance, they seem to contradict the idea that the initiative for assigning spiritual gifts is God's, not ours. But it is important to notice that neither of these verses is addressed to individual believers. Both refer to the church at Corinth as a whole, a church that had fallen into the particular error of elevating the gift of tongues above all other gifts. These verses need not be considered normative for us as individuals, but they are normative for our collective local congregations.

The second text is another related pair of verses, 1 Timothy 4:14 and 2 Timothy 1:6. In these verses, Paul states that Timothy received a gift by the laying on of hands, namely, Paul's hands and the hands of the presbytery or the elders. My understanding of this, in light of the many other Scriptures on the subject, is that the function of a presbytery is to lay on hands when the gift that God has given an individual is publicly recognized by the Body. This act of laying on of hands authorizes the person to minister through the gift in an official way. Whatever function other believers such as elders might have in *confirming* gifts, it must be remembered that the Spirit *distributes* gifts "as He wills" (1 Cor. 12:11).

THE BENEFITS OF SPIRITUAL GIFTS

What happens if you decide to discover, develop and use your spiritual gift or gifts?

Several things.

The Individual Grows

First of all, you will be a better Christian and better able to allow God to make your life count for Him. People who know their gifts have a handle on their spiritual job description, so to speak.

They find their place in the church with more ease. I have often said, half in jest, that one immediate benefit of the people in a church knowing their spiritual gifts is that the nominating committee can be phased out and a screening committee set up to receive applications for work. Things like this are happening, however. A while ago, for example, I received a letter from Pastor Paul Erickson of First Covenant Church of Portland, Oregon, who had been studying church growth in the Fuller Doctor of Ministry program. His letter said, "Our people have joined the exciting search for discovering and using their spiritual gifts. Six of our people contacted the nominating committee for service on the boards next year!"

When I was a member of Lake Avenue Church in Pasadena, California, we still had a nominating committee. But when the committee submitted their annual nominations to the congregation, each nominee had a brief biography, and the first item specifically listed their spiritual gifts. The idea behind that was that no one would occupy a position for which he or she had not been gifted by God.

Christian people who know their spiritual gifts tend to develop healthy self-esteem. This does not mean they "think more highly of themselves than they ought to think." However, they do learn that no matter what their gifts might be, they are important to God and to the Body. The ear learns not to say, "Because I am not an eye, I am not of the body" (1 Cor. 12:16). Crippling inferiority complexes drop by the wayside when people begin to "think soberly of themselves."

Humility is a chief Christian virtue, but like many good things, it can be overdone. Some Christians are so concerned about being humble that they render themselves virtually useless to the Body. This is a false humility, and it is often stimulated by an inferiority complex triggered by ignorance of spiritual gifts.

People who refuse to name their spiritual gifts on the grounds that they would be arrogant and presumptuous, only exhibit their failure to understand the biblical teaching on gifts. Some may have a less noble motive for not wanting to be associated with a particular gift—they might not want to be held accountable for its use. In that case, professed humility can be used as a cover-up for disobedience.

Most people who know their spiritual gifts and use them do not get bogged down by such negative attitudes. They first of all love God, they love their brothers and sisters, and they love themselves for what God has made them to be. They are not *proud* of their gifts, but they are *thankful* for them. They work together with other members of the Body in harmony and effectiveness.

The Whole Body Grows

Second, not only does knowing about spiritual gifts help individual Christians, but it also helps the Church as a whole. Ephesians 4 tells us that when spiritual gifts are in operation, the whole Body matures. It helps the Body to gain "the measure of the stature of the fullness of Christ" (v. 13).

When the church matures, predictably it grows. When the Body is functioning well and "each separate part works as it should, the whole body grows" (Eph. 4:16, *TEV*). Clearly, a biblical relationship between spiritual gifts and church growth exists. This whole book is intended to be an elaboration of how this relationship can work in practice.

God Is Glorified

The third and most important thing that knowing about spiritual gifts does is that it glorifies God. First Peter 4:10-11 advises

Christians to use their spiritual gifts, then adds the reason why: "That in all things God may be glorified through Jesus Christ, to whom belong the glory and the dominion forever and ever. Amen." What could be better than glorifying God? It is the "man's chief end," according to the Westminster Shorter Catechism, and most of us would agree.

STEWARDSHIP OF GIFTS: DANGERS AND DELIGHTS

The Bible tells us clearly and directly that Christians are stewards of their spiritual gifts (see 1 Pet. 4:10).

Stewardship, in the New Testament sense, is an awesome responsibility. Awesome, because the very notion of stewardship carries with it an important dimension of accountability.

According to 1 Corinthians 4:2, "It is required in stewards that one be found faithful." This verse has often been misinterpreted. I have heard people quote it and follow with the statement: "God doesn't require success; He just requires faithfulness." This kind of conclusion can become a pious excuse for laziness, blundering, incompetence or lack of courage. By no means is that what New Testament stewardship implies.

The key to stewardship is found in the parable of the talents in Matthew 25:14-30. Three stewards in the business world received different quantities of capital. Their responsibility was to use that resource for its assumed purpose in the business world—to make more money. Two of the three doubled their money, and when the day of accounting came, they were called "good and *faithful* servant[s]" (vv. 21,23). Faithfulness was directly related to success. The other steward was timid and a negative thinker. He could not recognize the potential of the resource he had. He did nothing with his capital, and thus was judged a "wicked and lazy servant" (v. 26).

Every spiritual gift we have is a resource that we must use and for which we will be held accountable at the judgment. Some will have one, some two and some five. The quantity to begin with does not matter. Stewards are responsible only for what the master has chosen to give them. But the resource that stewards have been given *must* be used to accomplish the *master's* purpose. Now is the time to prepare to answer that question each of us one day is going to hear from our Lord: "What did you do with the spiritual gift I entrusted to you?"

Tragically, many will not be able to answer that question. They will not be called "good and faithful servants," at least in that particular area of their lives, because they were ignorant of spiritual gifts. Ignorance, I repeat, is not bliss!

GIFTS CAN BE ABUSED

Spiritual gifts can be abused in many ways. United Methodist scholar Kenneth Kinghorn describes the extremes, using the colorful words "charisphobia" and "charismania."[9] Some who are fully aware of the potential of spiritual gifts can use them for acquiring power, gaining wealth, taking revenge or exploiting fellow believers. I will not attempt to expand on these or catalog all other abuses of spiritual gifts common today. But I do want to name and comment on two of them, which I consider to be especially widespread and counterproductive for church growth.

Gift Exaltation

The first abuse is *gift exaltation*. In some circles, it is popular to exalt one gift over the others. Having a certain gift constitutes a spiritual status symbol in some groups. The first-class citizens are separated from the second-class citizens on the basis of exercising a certain gift or gifts.

When this happens, gifts can easily become ends in themselves. They can glorify the user rather than the giver. They can benefit the individual rather than the Body. They can produce pride and self-indulgence. The Corinthians had fallen into this trap, and Paul writes 1 Corinthians 12-14 in an attempt to straighten them out. All of us need to take fair warning and avoid gift exaltation.

As I reviewed the literature on spiritual gifts, I found gift exaltation cropping up in unexpected places. One author, for example, calls prophecy the greatest gift. Another says that the greatest gift is the word of wisdom. Yet another suggests it might be apostleship. I myself do not believe any one gift is above all others, although we see a clear ordering of *offices* in 1 Corinthians 12:28, where Paul mentions first apostles, second prophets, third teachers and then other gifts follow, but not necessarily in order.

It seems that certain gifts may be more appropriate than others for certain occasions, for certain places, for certain philosophies of ministry, for certain groups and for certain tasks. In the Corinthian situation, prophecy was needed more than tongues, as 1 Corinthians 14 explains. This fact does not exalt a gift; it *orders* the gifts.

The Syndrome of Gift Projection

The second abuse is *gift projection*. Most Christians who have biographies written about themselves have accomplished extraordinary things during their lifetimes. What gave them the ability to turn in the kind of lifetime performance that would justify a biography? It has to be that God had given them a spiritual gift or gifts in an unusual degree, that they developed them conscientiously, and that they used them to the glory of God and for the benefit of the Body of Christ.

Few biographers, however, and few heroes of the biographies have been people sensitive to the biblical teaching on spiritual gifts. This has caused them to take another approach toward explaining the cause of their unusual feats. Unfortunately, the approach in such books tends toward consecration theology rather than gift theology. In other words, the idea comes across that so-and-so accomplished great exploits simply because he or she loved God so much. Ergo, if you loved God like that person did, dear reader, you could do the same thing. If you are not able to do these things, you now know the reason why. Something is wrong in your relationship to God.

Many Christians who read these biographies are, in fact, totally sold out to God. Consequently, they are often those who feel the most frustrated, guilty and defeated when they learn about these giants of the faith. To make matters worse, when the heroes of the biographies are ignorant of spiritual gifts, they sometimes engage in what I call gift projection. They tend to say, in honest humility, "Look, I'm just an ordinary Christian, no different from anyone else. Here's what I do, and God blesses it. If you just do what I do, God will bless you in the same way." What they rarely say, unfortunately, is, "I can do what I do because God has given me a spiritual gift. If you discover that God has given you the same, join me in this. If not, we will love and help each other as different members of the Body."

People caught up in the syndrome of gift projection seem to want the whole Body to be an eye. They unwittingly impose guilt and shame on fellow Christians. They cause those who might be feet to say, "Because I am not a hand, I am not of the body" (1 Cor. 12:15). They usually have little idea how devastating gift projection can be for those who have different gifts. They are like the steward in the parable who came back with 10 talents saying to the one who came back with 4, "If you only loved the master more, you would have come back with 10 also," without mentioning that the master gave him 5 talents to start with but gave the other only 2.

People who employ gift projection not only can impose a guilt trip on others, but more seriously they also fail to recognize that the reason others are different from them and may have 2 talents instead of 5 is that the Holy Spirit Himself has distributed "to each one individually as *He wills*" (1 Cor. 12:11). In a way, they are calling into question the wisdom and sovereignty of God at that point. They may be indulging in the "creator complex"—intent on making others over in their own image.

George Müller of Bristol, England, for example, has been called the apostle of faith. A number of biographies have been written about him, describing the way God worked through him to care for orphans about 100 years ago. I have read some of them, and I have to say that George Müller would undoubtedly be listed in the *Guinness Book of Spiritual World Records*, if such a book were ever published. He had other gifts as well, but one of his greatest was the gift of faith. Müller, however, as far as I know, never recognized this as a spiritual gift. At a high point in one of these biographies, when readers are appropriately dazzled by his spiritual feats, Mr. Müller says, "Let not Satan deceive you in making you think you could not have the same faith, but that it is only for persons situated as I am. . . . I pray to the Lord and expect an answer to my requests; and may not you do the same, dear believing reader?"[10]

At one point earlier in my Christian life, I used to read a lot of biographies. Then I stopped almost completely and at first did not know why. What I did know is that, while they were enjoyable reading, when I finished I felt miserable. I always felt that "if so-and-so can do it, so should I." Now I guess I know why I stopped reading them—I did not like feeling miserable! The "dear believing reader" bit got to me. I was an unsuspecting victim of gift projection, and because I was still operating out of the assumptions of consecration theology rather than gift theology, I did not know how to handle it.

In the chapters that follow, as we deal with specific gifts, I will refer back from time to time to the syndrome of gift projection. Not only do I have strong personal feelings about it, but I also believe that in many cases it is hindering church growth.

It is time now to get specific about the 28 individual gifts.

REFLECTIONS

1. *The* most basic step for a Christian in discovering God's plan for life is to discover his or her spiritual gift or gifts. Do you think this is an overstatement?

2. For some, the idea that the church should be seen as an organism rather than an organization is new. Discuss the differences between the two.

3. Obviously, women have spiritual gifts. Do you think God gives all the gifts to women? If not, which ones would He withhold?

4. Some, like Gene Getz, argue that believers should not be admonished to discover their own spiritual gifts. Peter Wagner disagrees. If you are meeting in a small group, discuss the differences between the two positions and then define where you stand.

5. Do you know anyone who indulges in gift projection? Why can this do harm to others?

Notes

1. The Barna Group, "Awareness of Spiritual Gifts Is Changing," *The Barna Update*, February 5, 2001. http://www.barna.org/FlexPage.aspx?Page= BarnaUpdate&BarnaUpdateID=81 (accessed December 10, 2004).

2. Hereafter, italics in quoted Scripture passages are added by the author for emphasis.

3. John MacArthur, Jr., *The Church, the Body of Christ* (Grand Rapids, MI: Zondervan Publishing House, 1973), p. 136.

4. W. T. Purkiser, *The Gifts of the Spirit* (Kansas City, MO: Beacon Hill Press, 1975), p. 21.

5. Nancy Hardesty, "Gifts," *The Other Side* (July-August 1977), p. 40.

6. Elizabeth O'Connor, *Eighth Day of Creation: Gifts and Creativity* (Dallas: Word Books, 1971), p. 15.

7. Gene A. Getz develops this point in two of his works. The earlier is *Sharpening the Focus of the Church* (Chicago: Moody Press, 1974), pp. 112-117; and the later is *Building Up One Another* (Wheaton, IL: Victor Books, 1976), pp. 9-16.

8. Getz, *Building Up One Another*, p. 9.

9. Kenneth Cain Kinghorn, *Gifts of the Spirit* (Nashville, TN: Abingdon Press, 1976), p. 95.

10. Basil Miller, *George Muller: The Man of Faith* (Grand Rapids, MI: Zondervan Publishing House, 1941), p. 58.

Chapter 3

WHAT THE GIFTS ARE: AN OPEN-ENDED APPROACH

Before we discuss any more of the implications that spiritual gifts have for the health of your church, we need to be as specific as we can about what the gifts really are and which ones are available for individuals and churches today.

My approach to this is going to be as open-ended as possible. Because, as we will see in some detail, the Bible does not lock us into tight restrictions about the number of gifts, this seems to be a legitimate procedure. My intention is to do this in such a way that any church that wants to use spiritual gifts to help it grow will be able to fit in.

I think this can be done because I believe so strongly in the universality of spiritual gifts. Every Christian has them and every church has them. Many may still be buried in the ground, as was the talent in Matthew 25, but they don't need to stay buried. They can and should be unearthed and used for the glory of God and for the growth of the Church. Spiritual gifts are for Methodist churches and for Conservative Baptist churches. They are for Holiness churches and for Pentecostal churches. They are for open-theism churches and for Calvinistic churches. They are for house churches and for megachurches, for suburban churches and for inner-city churches, for African-

American churches and for Hispanic churches. They are for churches that use *The Scofield Reference Bible* and for churches that use the *New International Version*. They are for every church of which Christ is the head and the members are parts of His Body.

PRODUCING EFFECTIVE MINISTRY

Spiritual gifts work. They actually produce effective ministry. When they do not, something is wrong with the Body's health. If the Bible is clear about anything, it is clear that (1) God wants every Christian to have and to use a spiritual gift or gifts and that (2) He wants His lost sheep to be found and His Church to grow. Spiritual gifts are utilitarian. They are functional. They have a task to do, and if they are working properly, the task will be accomplished. When the gifts work together in a church that wants to grow and the church is willing to pay the price for growth, the church will see God's blessing, and it should grow because it will be healthy.

As the book progresses, I am going to describe 28 different spiritual gifts. This is no hard-and-fast number. There may be more; there may be fewer. I will explain this variation as we go along.

The order in which I have chosen to describe the gifts needs to be understood. Some books on spiritual gifts list them in the order in which they appear in the Bible. Others describe them as subpoints under several major classifications. At least one book deals with them in alphabetical order. In this book, however, I will discuss each gift as it naturally comes up and needs to be emphasized for its particular contribution to the growth and health of the Church. In this chapter, for example, I will list all 28 gifts but will discuss only 5. In the next chapter, I will discuss 4 more and so on. To help you find your way around, a special directory in the front of the book lists where each gift is located for its principal discussion. The appendix at the end of the book lists the gifts with a concise definition for each one. You may consult the index for additional references to the gifts throughout the book.

THE THREE KEY LISTS

The great majority of the spiritual gifts mentioned in the Bible are found in three key chapters: Romans 12, 1 Corinthians 12 and Ephesians 4. Mark these three locations in your Bible for future reference because they are primary. Several secondary chapters also provide other important details: 1 Corinthians 7; 13–14; Ephesians 3; and 1 Peter 4.

I will begin putting the master list of gifts together by using the three primary chapters. The words in parentheses are variant translations found in several English versions of the Bible.

Romans 12 mentions the following spiritual gifts:

1. Prophecy (preaching, inspired utterance)
2. Service (ministry)
3. Teaching
4. Exhortation (stimulating faith, encouraging)
5. Giving (contributing, generosity, sharing)
6. Leadership (authority, ruling)
7. Mercy (sympathy, comfort to the sorrowing, showing kindness)

First Corinthians 12 adds (without repeating those already listed from Romans):

8. Wisdom (wise advice, wise speech)

9. Knowledge (studying, speaking with knowledge)
10. Faith
11. Healing
12. Miracles (doing great deeds)
13. Discerning of spirits (discrimination in spiritual matters)
14. Tongues (speaking in languages never learned, ecstatic utterance)
15. Interpretation of tongues
16. Apostle
17. Helps
18. Administration (governments, getting others to work together)

Ephesians 4 adds (again, without repeating any of the above):

19. Evangelist
20. Pastor (caring for God's people)

CHURCH OFFICES AND THE PETER PRINCIPLE

Some may notice that the list in Ephesians 4 is slightly different from the other two, because it mentions *offices* rather than the underlying *gifts* as such. This is correct. When it speaks of apostles, prophets, evangelists, pastors and teachers—referred to by some as the fivefold ministry—being given to the Church (see v. 11), the focus is directed toward individuals who have been recognized in such official positions. Usually such people have been ordained or commissioned with a public laying on of hands. For the most part, they would probably be considered as members of the church or denominational or parachurch professional staff.

Christian churches today vary considerably about which offices are recognized. Some churches believe that Ephesians 4:11 locks them into those five, and some take a further cue from the pastoral Epistles, which also mention elders and deacons and bishops, and some go beyond this. A growing number of churches officially recognize the offices of apostles and prophets, whereas others, such as Presbyterian, Assemblies of God and Nazarene churches, recognize neither of these. But Nazarenes do have offices of evangelist and general superintendent and district superintendent. Southern Baptist churches call their district superintendents executive secretaries of state conventions; the Church of God (Cleveland) calls them state overseers; and Seventh-day Adventist churches call them conference presidents. People in charge of local churches are variously called pastors, ministers or priests. The Salvation Army gives military labels to their officers: lieutenants, captains and colonels. And we could go on.

Whatever the nomenclature for church offices, it is interesting to observe that the spiritual gifts are given by grace, but the offices themselves are earned by works. For example, a pastoral ordination committee does not presume to give the candidate the gift of pastor. The committee is established to judge whether the candidate, who presumably has been given the gift of pastor by God, has sufficiently exhibited the fruit of that gift in his or her ministry. If not, the committee is obligated to withhold ordination into the office of pastor.

The main purpose of discussing the differences here is to point out that regardless of what the office is named, the person who is called, ordained, commissioned or licensed to fill that office should qualify for it on the basis of the particular spiritual gift-mix God has given to him or her. The apostle ought to have the gift of apostle, the prophet the gift of prophecy, the evangelist the gift of evangelism and so forth.

Herein lies a persistent growth problem in American church-es. People are often allowed to occupy local church or denominational offices with little or no reference to whether or not they have the appropriate spiritual gifts. Unfortunately, church offices are often awarded on the basis of seniority, influence, personality, political manipulation, education, prestige, rotation or all of the above. I am afraid that the Peter Principle is more rampant in our churches than it ought to be. For those not familiar with the Peter Principle, it was first articulated by best-selling author Laurence Peter. His principle states: "In a hierarchy every employee tends to rise to his level of incompetence."[1] The final promotion for any person is predictably from a level of competence to a level of incompetence, and there the person usually stops. They are promoted no more. Most of Peter's illustrations come from business, government and industry, but he could just as easily have illustrated the principle from the Church.

Laurence Peter laments that in government and industry the principle is almost inexorable and, alas, our society is unnecessarily doomed to a degree of incompetence and mediocrity. But this need not and ought not to be the state of affairs in the Church. God did not design the Church for mediocrity. He knew about the Peter Principle before Laurence Peter was born, and He designed a system to avoid it. If we only would decide to fill our church offices strictly on the basis of recognized spiritual gifts, the Peter Principle would never victimize us. And we would unlock tremendous potential for growth that is now largely dormant and wasting away.

One of the greatest obstacles to growth today is that so many churches assign members to vacant church positions on the basis of their *availability* rather than their *giftedness*. This needs to be changed.

COMPLETING **THE MASTER LIST**

The three primary lists give us 20 separate gifts.

One thing becomes immediately evident just from looking at the three primary lists—none of the lists is complete in itself. Some gifts mentioned in Ephesians are mentioned in Romans, and some in Romans are mentioned in 1 Corinthians, and some in 1 Corinthians are mentioned in Ephesians. Apparently, none of them is intended to be a complete catalog of the gifts that God gives. And we could surmise that if none of the three lists is complete in itself, then the three lists together are probably not complete.

The Bible itself confirms that this is a correct assumption. At least five other gifts are mentioned in the New Testament:

21. Celibacy (continence)
22. Voluntary poverty
23. Martyrdom
24. Hospitality
25. Missionary

I will postpone discussing voluntary poverty and the missionary gift, because they come up more naturally in other contexts. But at this point I do want to take a closer look at the other three, because they will teach us some valuable lessons needed just at this point.

THE GIFT OF **CELIBACY**

Some adult Christians are married; some are single. Obviously, more are married than are single, and we know that this is the way that God designed the human race. Some single Christian adults (not all, to be sure) are single because God has given them the spiritual gift of celibacy. God has so constituted them that by remaining single, they can better accomplish His will for their lives.

> *The gift of celibacy is the special ability that God gives to certain members of the Body of Christ to remain single and enjoy it and not suffer undue sexual temptations.*

If you are single, and know down in your heart that you would get married in an instant if a reasonable opportunity presented itself, you probably do not have the gift of celibacy. If you are single and find yourself terribly frustrated by unfulfilled sexual impulses, you probably do not have the gift. But if neither of these things seems to bother you and you really feel good about being single, rejoice—you probably have found one of your spiritual gifts.

The biblical text for this is found in 1 Corinthians 7:7. Here Paul discusses his own condition of celibacy and calls it a charisma, a spiritual gift. Men and women who are celibate are part of God's plan for His people, and they should be accepted and honored as such. As I will detail in a moment, Paul goes on in the chapter to explain some of the tremendous advantages of the gift of celibacy.

Notice that no special gift is necessary to get married, have sexual relations and raise a family. God has made humans with organs, glands and passions so that the majority of people, Christians included, normally get married, and most are supposed to do just that.

Advantages of Celibacy

Men and women who have the gift of celibacy have tremendous advantages. Paul emphasizes these in 1 Corinthians 7. Here he mentions, for example, that Christians who have the gift of celibacy can actually serve the Lord better than those who do not, because they do not have to worry about how to please their husband or wife or family (see 1 Cor. 7:32-34). I have found this true in my own experience. It became more vivid after I developed a personal friendship with John Stott, one of today's most respected Bible teachers, authors and Christian leaders. John Stott and I served together for years on the executive committee of the Lausanne Committee for World Evangelization, so we met frequently in various parts of the world, enjoyed fellowship with each other and shared many areas of mutual interest.

John Stott is one who has the gift of celibacy, and because this is of special interest to me, I have observed the advantages he has over others who, like me, do not. For one thing, I make it a habit to call home frequently when I am traveling. If I spend too much time traveling, I hear about it in kindly, but firm, ways. When I am home, I give high priority to setting aside time to spend with my family. I plan dinner at home, Saturdays working around the house and yard, and days out for sporting events and other entertainment. Whenever possible, Doris travels with me. We set aside special times to visit our children and .grandchildren.

While I am busy caring for my growing extended family, John Stott is writing another book, planning another conference, preparing another lecture or traveling to another country. No wonder I cannot come near to keeping up with his literary output. He has written so many books that some Christian bookstores now feature a special John Stott rack!

I Need My Wife

Do I envy John Stott? Not in the least. If I did, I would be untrue to what the Bible teaches about spiritual gifts. I cannot thank

God enough for the outstanding contribution that John is making to building up Christians and to the task of world evangelization. And me? I would not trade my wife and family for a hundred special Peter Wagner racks in Christian bookstores! In fact, because I do not have the gift of celibacy, I can categorically affirm that without my wife and what she contributes to every area of my being, the work I attempt to do for the Lord would be a disaster.

The temptation of gift projection (see chapter 2) is not frequent among those having the gift of celibacy. The celibate of whom I am aware has come closest to it, believe it or not, is the apostle Paul. In 1 Corinthians 7, Paul gets so enthusiastic about the advantages he finds in being single (evidence shows he was a widower at the time, according to many biblical scholars) that he says, "I wish that all men were even as I myself" (v. 7). But then, under the Spirit's further inspiration, he catches himself and quickly adds that he knows it really is a spiritual gift.

One more aspect of the gift of celibacy needs to be noted. Celibacy is one of the two gifts that cannot stand alone. (The other is the missionary gift, which I will explain later on.) In other words, no merit exists whatsoever in being unmarried if that is all there is to it. Being unmarried should allow a man or woman to be more effective in the use of whatever other gift or gift-mix God gives to the person. The gift of celibacy must always be understood and used in the light of what else it will help the person to accomplish in ministry.

EVERY GIFT IS IN THE MINORITY

This discussion of celibacy raises an important general principle relating to spiritual gifts: More members of the Body of Christ *do not* share a particular spiritual gift than those who *do*. More

Christians, as I have just pointed out, do not have the gift of celibacy than have it. Likewise, more Christians do not have the gift of pastor than have it. The same applies to prophecy, evangelism, teacher, hospitality and probably every other gift on the list.

The analogy of the physical body that Paul firmly establishes in Romans 12:4 as the model through which we are to understand spiritual gifts clarifies this. We know that in our own human bodies, the majority of members are not hands. More members are not eyes, kidneys, toes, teeth or elbows than are. God has determined that we are supposed to have two eyes, and this is exactly enough to do the job of seeing on behalf of the hundreds of other members of the same body. Tongues and

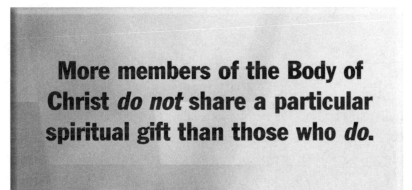

More members of the Body of Christ *do not* share a particular spiritual gift than those who *do*.

hips, for example, do not need to see, because the eyes see for them. The Bible says specifically that the whole body should not be an eye, because if it were, it could not hear or smell (see 1 Cor. 12:17).

The same applies to the Body of Christ. The Shakers, for example, made the mistake of universalizing the gift of celibacy, not allowing church members to get married. As a result, they died a natural death as a denomination. Not only did they cut off biological growth, but transfer and conversion growth also became uninviting possibilities for them. Their lifestyle could not appeal to many people, mainly because God has not made many people that way. The Catholic Church also has perpetuated an unbiblical application of gifts by requiring all clergy to remain single whether they have the gift of celibacy or not.

It is reasonable to conclude that something less than 50 percent of the Body should be expected to have any particular gift. My hunch is that, when the facts are known, most of the percentages will come out far less than 50 percent. I have been able to do some research on the gift of evangelist and found that the figure is less than 10 percent, probably nearer to 5 percent. The gift of missionary is only maybe 1 percent, and intercession around 5 percent. More research will undoubtedly uncover ratios for other gifts.

THE GIFT OF MARTYRDOM

Although 1 Corinthians 13 is known mostly as a chapter on love, it also has two brief lists of spiritual gifts (see vv. 1-3,8). Most of them are picked up and repeated from chapter 12, but two—voluntary poverty and martyrdom—become new additions to the list. Martyrdom is expressed in the words "though I give my body to be burned" (v. 3).

What is the gift of martyrdom? Once in a while I say in jest that it is the gift you use only once! But really it is broader than just dying for the faith. It is an attitude toward suffering and death that is quite unusual. The inbuilt law of human self-preservation is characteristic of most people, Christians as well as non-Christians. The average Christian does not welcome thoughts of persecution, suffering, torture or being murdered. Most think they could take it if it came, but they certainly would not welcome it, and they would make every effort to avoid it if possible.

> *The gift of martyrdom is a special ability that God gives to certain members of the Body of Christ to undergo suffering for the faith even to death while consistently displaying a joyous and victorious attitude that brings glory to God.*

When death is imminent, even though there might be a possibility of escaping, the person having the gift of martyrdom may well choose to suffer and die. Christians who have other gifts and feel that God wants them to continue to use them, but who do not have the gift of martyrdom, will usually choose to flee.

This exact situation presented itself to my dear friend Festo Kivengere, who was at the time a colleague on the Lausanne Committee for World Evangelization. During Idi Amin's reign of terror in Uganda, Festo Kivengere was a prominent and influential bishop of an Anglican diocese. In 1977, he raised his voice in protest when Amin ordered Kivengere's beloved friend and archbishop, Janani Luwum, to be murdered. As a result, Kivengere ended up high on Amin's hit list. He and his wife decided that they did not have the gift of martyrdom, and they fled for their lives. Their hair-raising tale of escape is told in Bishop Kivengere's touching book *I Love Idi Amin*.[2] They moved to the United States, where the unusual gifts of exhortation and evangelism that God had given to Festo Kivengere were preserved for the blessing of God's kingdom and the cause of world evangelization until Kivengere died a natural death.

Only recently have I come to appreciate fully the gift of martyrdom. When my wife, Doris, and I first went to Bolivia as missionaries in 1956, we were stationed in the tiny Chiquitano Indian village of Santiago de Chiquitos. From this village, 13 years previously, five New Tribes missionaries had headed off into the jungle to contact the Ayoré Indians and were never seen again.

George Haight, our senior missionary, knew the area and the people as did few others. He had said to the New Tribes missionaries, "If you do not take guns, you will not come back alive." They replied that they would prefer death for the glory of God rather than carry firearms. This was not a spur-of-the-moment decision. I made a point to study their lives, their letters and their magazine articles, because I was writing a book on the Ayorés several years after the tribe had been contacted and were being evangelized. At first glance, I came to the hasty and immature conclusion that the five had suffered from a martyr complex. I now see it differently. Both they and their wives were faithfully exercising a spiritual gift. The book telling their story, *God Planted Five Seeds,* which was written by one of the widows, expresses well the attitude of people who have the gift of martyrdom.[3]

In contrast, missionary George Haight did not have the gift of martyrdom. A battle-scarred member of the Canadian cavalry in World War I, his policy was to carry guns at all times and to use them if necessary. On one of the unsuccessful expeditions to search for the missing five, the Ayorés engaged Haight and his party in a jungle battle, and Haight shot and killed an Indian in self-defense.[4] He told me later that he believed that in the total economy of God, his life would count more over the next 20 years than that of the Ayoré. God blessed him. He and his wife, Helen, were dearly loved by the people of the area for the selfless exercise of their gifts of service, helps, administration and missionary. He died of natural causes in 1978.

Stephen, of the church at Jerusalem, was one who died a martyr's death. We may not have enough evidence to know for sure if he had the gift of martyrdom, although his last words, "Lord, do not charge them with this sin" (Acts 7:60), may carry a hint that he did. But we do know that his death resulted in tremendously accelerated church growth through Judea, Samaria and even to the Gentiles in Antioch.

I could not say what percentage of believers has the gift of martyrdom. However, it may be more than we think. David Barrett's research indicates that since 1950 approximately 278,000 Christians have given their lives for their faith every year.[5]

THE GIFT OF HOSPITALITY

The biblical text for the gift of hospitality is admittedly somewhat imprecise. First Peter 4:9 says, "Be hospitable to one another without grumbling," and then verse 10 immediately speaks of spiritual gifts. One legitimate way of interpreting the juxtaposition of the two verses is to understand that the use of hospitality is mentioned in verse 9, and then attached to verse 10 by using a "just as" word, so that it could well be paraphrased, "Use hospitality, just as all Christians have received any other spiritual gift."

If this seems to be stretching the text, I would suggest that, even so, hospitality should be listed as a spiritual gift whether or not it was so mentioned in the Bible. I will give other illustrations of this principle shortly. But meanwhile, hospitality means, "love of strangers," and some people undoubtedly have a special ability to love strangers for the glory of God. What is the gift of hospitality?

The gift of hospitality is the special ability that God gives to certain members of the Body of Christ to provide an open house and warm welcome for those in need of food and lodging.[6]

Not only do those with the gift have the skills to offer warm hospitality, but they also love to do it. Although it seems incredible to those of us who do not have the gift, people who have the gift of hospitality are happier having guests in their home than being alone. This is a supernatural ability given to relatively few. Most people who do not have the gift find it a drag and a nuisance to have outsiders around their house for anything but short and well-monitored visits.

Hospitality Before Pride

One person who has discovered that she has the gift of hospitality is author Karen Mains. She has written a book about hospitality, *Open Heart, Open Home*.[7] In an article on the subject in *Moody* magazine, she says, "True hospitality is a gift of the Spirit," and explains that she received supernatural help for "creating heart-to-heart human bonds."[8] The motto of a person who has this gift is Hospitality before pride; and it is quickly evident to others who enter such a home.

When guests are invited in, most people who do not have the gift of hospitality want everything to be in place, rugs clean, furniture dusted, toys and newspapers picked up, fresh-cut flowers on the tables, candlelight and the food something special, prepared and served just right. That is the way it invariably is when Doris and I have guests over, for example. To be honest, we do enjoy a neat, well-appointed home, and we want our guests to see it the way we believe it should be at its best. Maybe this could be interpreted as a sort of "pride before hospitality."

But people who have the gift of hospitality do not see it as we do. Karen Mains tells how she is able to welcome a woman into her "unsightly rooms," and she refuses to embarrass her guest by apologizing. She finds it uplifting, and describes it well in books and articles.

Feeling at Home

Those of us in the Body who do not have the gift of hospitality certainly are thankful for those who do. As missionaries on furlough, my family and I were frequently in the homes of fellow Christians who had the gift of hospitality. After a little experience, we could tell immediately which of the hosts had the gift. One of the outstanding couples who frequently cared for us were Glen and Irene Main of Bell, California. Whenever we were in their house, we felt completely at home. Because they had the gift of hospitality and because those with the gift always have the comfort of the visitor as their highest priority, the Mains on one occasion went out and purchased a family car when they knew I was coming home from Bolivia for a while. They gave me the keys to the car when I got off the plane. They began using the car themselves only after I left again for Bolivia. We have many other friends, just as close to us and just as consecrated Christians and just as supportive of missionaries, who would never do such a thing, nor would they be expected to. They have other gifts that Glen and Irene Main may not have. The Body needs them all.

Because the gift of hospitality is such a beautiful gift and so sincerely admired, those who have it need to be careful to avoid gift projection. I once visited L'Abri in Switzerland where Francis and Edith Schaeffer operated a wonderful center for the spiritual renewal of troubled Christian young people. An atmosphere of hospitality oozed from every nook and cranny. When I arrived, I immediately sensed that one of the two, if not both, must have the gift of hospitality.

Then I later read an article by Edith Schaeffer in *Christianity Today* in which she described her attitude toward hospitality.[9] Unfortunately, the article did not indicate that she recognized she had special help from God to do what she was doing. The article's title, "Hospitality: Optional or Commanded?" set the tone. As I read along, I thought she might have been indulging in gift projection, suggesting that other Christians who do not show L'Abri kind of hospitality may be something short of "doers of the Word, and not hearers only," as she states. If I did not know about spiritual gifts, I might have allowed the article to make me feel guilty. It didn't.

Cultural Biases

The growth of the Church in the Roman Empire in New Testament times was heavily dependent upon hospitality.[10] The exercise of hospitality was a cultural institution, essential for those who traveled, as did the Christian missionaries. It was far different from travel conditions today with motels, hotels, rental cars and credit cards. When I travel for seminars, I request a single room in a hotel. All the demands involved in staying in someone's private home are an excessive drain on my energies and unnecessary in our American culture. When I travel abroad, however, it is a different story. Many cultures in the Third World are closer to that of the first-century Roman Empire than ours in the United States, and hospitality there is more essential to the growth of the Church. I believe that the distribution of some spiritual gifts has cultural biases and that, consequently, we would predictably find a higher percentage of Christians who have the gift of hospitality in Nigeria, for example, than in the United States. And those in Nigeria without the gift would have a higher expectation placed on them for entertaining guests than we would expect in our more mechanized and individualized culture. In the first century, bishops and widows in particular were expected to be good at hospitality (see 1 Tim. 3:2; 5:9-10).

Hospitality is useful for church growth in America today when (1) evangelistic outreach is geared around evangelistic Bible studies that meet in homes and (2) a church's philosophy of ministry includes multiplying home cell groups, as several successful, growing churches in the United States are currently demonstrating. The gift of hospitality can also be used well for hosting social events in the church facilities or by greeters on Sunday mornings.

ARE ALL GIFTS MENTIONED IN THE BIBLE?

Because none of the three primary lists is complete in itself, and the three lists together are not complete, it is reasonable to conclude that the list of all the 25 gifts mentioned in the Bible may not be complete either.

I was gratified when I read the works of several other scholars who agree. Others suggest adding three gifts that I have chosen *not* to add, namely craftsmanship, preaching and writing. But I have decided to add three others, I repeat, not because I can cite a Bible verse indicating that they are gifts (even though they are biblical ministries), but because my empirical observation of church life and ministry leads me to the conclusion. They are

26. Intercession
27. Deliverance (exorcism)
28. Leading worship

This is what I mean when I say that I prefer an open-ended approach to the spiritual gifts. For example, in the first two editions of this book, I listed 27 gifts, but I always had a lingering feeling that I should have included leading worship. In this third edition, therefore, I have decided to model open-endedness by adding a twenty-eighth gift.

Because deliverance (exorcism) is closely related to the gift of discernment of spirits, I prefer to discuss the two of them together in another chapter. But for now let's take a brief look at the gift of intercession and the gift of leading worship.

THE GIFT OF INTERCESSION

As I have mentioned, I have postulated that there is such a thing as the gift of intercession, not because I know of a biblical text for it, but because it is a biblical ministry, and I believe I have seen it in action. Certain Christians, it seems to me, have the gift of intercession.

> *The gift of intercession is the special ability that God gives to certain members of the Body of Christ to pray for extended periods of time on a regular basis and see frequent and specific answers to their prayers to a degree much greater than that which is expected of the average Christian.*

Because not many other authors on spiritual gifts refer to this gift, I was encouraged when I read that Elizabeth O'Connor recognized it in the Church of the Savior in Washington, D.C. She tells of a lady who came into one of the groups of their church and whom "the group had no difficulty in confirming as an intercessor. Confirmation of her gift did not mean that the rest of us would give up our prayers of intercession for each other and the group and its mission, but it did mean that we now had a person who would spend more time at the work of intercession."[11]

Because intercession has not been widely regarded as a gift, many Christians tend not to recognize it when it comes along. If prayer is as important as we think it is, I find it curious that churches have not added staff members to give themselves to intercession—other staff is employed for just about everything else. More seminaries ought to offer courses in prayer. Asbury Seminary is the first I know of to designate a professor of prayer and enroll students who are majoring in prayer. Campus Crusade for Christ believes strongly in prayer, strongly enough to assign the responsibility to the founding president's wife, Vonette Bright. They have several full-time staff members in their prayer-care ministry who go to the prayer chapel, pray for eight hours and call it another day's work.[12]

The life of Rees Howells, a Welsh coal miner who was obviously given the gift of intercession, is instructive reading for those who might want to learn more about it. In the book *Rees Howells: Intercessor*, author Norman Grubb points out that an intercessor is something more than an ordinary Christian who intensifies his or her prayer life. Intercession involves a combination of identification, agony and authority that those without the gift will seldom experience or even understand.[13]

In 1987, I began serious research on prayer. By then God had given Doris and me firsthand contact with people with the gift of intercession. Today, in our rather widespread ministry responsibilities for global prayer, we work closely with intercessors day in and day out. My book *Prayer Shield* deals with the gift of intercession at considerable length.

In *Prayer Shield*, I develop a detailed profile of those who have the gift of intercession. Here I will only outline the high points:

- They pray longer than most. A minimum is one hour a day, but more commonly they average two to five hours of praying per day.

- They pray with more intensity.
- They enjoy prayer more and get great personal satisfaction from praying.
- They see more frequent and dramatic answers to their prayers.
- They hear from God more regularly and more accurately than most.[14]

As far as I have been able to test, around 5 percent of the members of a healthy church might have the gift of intercession. They will often do some 80 percent of the effective praying in the life of the congregation. And we also find that around 8 out of 10 intercessors are women. Just as some gifts seem to be culture biased, other gifts seem to be gender biased.

How can those who have the gift of intercession contribute to the growth and health of their church? I have also researched this extensively and reported my findings in a companion volume to *Prayer Shield*, called *Churches That Pray*. In it, I mention my friend Archie Parrish, who did some significant testing while he was on the staff of Coral Ridge Presbyterian Church in Fort Lauderdale, Florida.

At Coral Ridge, a large and growing church, the Evangelism Explosion program had long been a potent force for outreach and growth. But in 1976, Archie Parrish introduced a further improvement that worked so well it was recommended to all churches using Evangelism Explosion. Two church members who were not on the Evangelism Explosion team were asked to volunteer to pray for each Evangelism Explosion worker on a regular basis, but especially on Tuesday nights when the workers were out witnessing. The evangelist was responsible to get in touch with the two intercessors each week to report the results and give prayer requests. After this started, the number of professions of faith immediately increased by an astounding 100 percent!

Prayer for church growth has power. Thousands who have the special gift of prayer need to discover, develop and use this gift. When they do, other gifted people will find themselves much more effective in whatever their particular ministry might be, and the Body will become healthy and grow.

THE GIFT OF LEADING WORSHIP

Those who have the spiritual gift of leading congregations in worship are something more than good musicians. True, they will have attained a satisfactory level of musical ability, but it does not necessarily follow that the better the musician, the better the worship leader. This is why I did not follow the suggestions of some other authors on spiritual gifts to add the gift of music to the list. I think it is more accurate to call it the gift of leading worship.

Worship leader Ron Kenoly agrees. He says, "[God] wants us to create a place where He can come and receive from us whatever's in our hearts—it's not just the music. He's looking for heart expressions that will manifest themselves in songs."[15]

Who can be used by God to "create a place," which Ron Kenoly talks about? Not any church member at all. Not every pastor. Not necessarily a choir member or a guitarist in the worship band. Not even, sad to say, every church music director. No, the Holy Spirit must initiate this, but He will do it by giving a spiritual gift of leading worship to individuals whom He chooses.

Here is how worship leader Tim Hughes expresses it: "Our worship needs to be Spirit led; in fact, I would go so far as to say that the Holy Spirit should be our worship leader. Therefore, leading worship is not just a case of throwing a few favorite songs together. If we go to God on our own terms, not His, we can miss out on the Holy Spirit's plan for a meeting."[16]

> *The gift of leading worship is the special ability that God gives to certain members of the Body of Christ to accurately discern the heart of God for a particular public worship service, to draw others into an intimate experience of God during the worship time and to allow the Holy Spirit to change directions and emphases as the service progresses.*

None of this, of course, would be meant to imply that musical ability is not a great asset to a worship leader. Since our public worship mostly centers around singing, it would be hard to imagine a tone-deaf worship leader. The best worship leaders are good musicians. They also need to know how to assemble and lead choirs and bands. In some churches, they must choose who will play the piano or the pipe organ. If they are ministering through a spiritual gift, the Holy Spirit will have given them the ability to manage these tasks to the approval and satisfaction of all concerned.

The definition speaks of allowing the Holy Spirit to change directions as the service progresses. I, for one, greatly admire this ability in the best worship leaders. As I have been observing worship leaders with this book on spiritual gifts in mind, I have realized how insensitive I, as an average church worshiper, can be to what is actually happening spiritually to the congregation as a whole during worship. It takes a gifted worship leader to know. In his book *Here I Am to Worship*, Tim Hughes allows us to peek into this area of his discernment. He speaks of some "disasters" that he has experienced, and goes on to say, "There have been times when I've felt God has put on my heart a line to sing, so I sing it out again and again—yet no one really responds.

Occasionally I've gone into spontaneous times of worship and have left everyone behind because it was Tim led rather than Spirit led."[17] My point in quoting this is that most of us would probably have gone home after church those days and never given a second thought to what happened in worship. Not a true worship leader. A true worship leader would have spent considerable time asking God not to allow it to happen again.

HYPHENATED GIFTS

Some books on spiritual gifts make a point that in Ephesians 4:11 the gifts most often listed as "pastor" and "teacher" should really be translated "pastor-teacher." William McRae, for example, says, "This gift is the only dual gift in the New Testament. There are not two gifts here. It is one gift which has two distinct dimensions."[18] This could be correct, at least in the translation that best reflects the sense of the Greek text.

In an open-ended approach to spiritual gifts, however, I have found it best to consider many other hyphenated gifts that are at work in the Body of Christ. Because pastor-teacher is indeed a very common combination of gifts, it stands as our prototype. Most scholars would admit that teacher can stand alone as a gift because it actually does in some of the other lists. Ephesians 4:11 is the only list that mentions pastor in combination with teacher. It is true that in a sense, a pastor has to be "able to teach" (1 Tim. 3:2). But whether all of this means every pastor needs the gift of teaching or that every teacher needs the gift of pastor is doubtful. In fact, I am quite sure that I have both the gift and the office of teacher, but I am equally sure that I do not have the gift of pastor.

As we continue to discuss the gifts in context, I will be mentioning several other common hyphenated gifts, such as intercession-healing, tongues-interpretation, giving-voluntary poverty, pastor-exhortation, apostle-leadership, discernment-deliverance and so forth. But at this point we simply need to become familiar with the hyphenated gift concept and know that it is not limited to pastor-teacher.

VARIATIONS AND DEGREES OF GIFTS

Within almost every one of the 28 spiritual gifts will be found a wide range of variations and degrees. The cue for this might be seen in 1 Corinthians 12:4-6, where it speaks of gifts (*charismaton*), ministries (*diakonion*) and activities (*energematon*). Ray Stedman defines ministry as "the sphere in which a gift is performed," and an activity (or working) as "the degree of power by which a gift is manifested or ministered on a specific occasion."[19]

A person who has the gift of evangelist, for example, might be a personal evangelist or a public evangelist—different ministries within the same gift. One public evangelist might be an international celebrity who fills stadiums with 50,000 people and sees 3,000 conversions in a week. Another public evangelist might minister mostly in churches that hold 500 people and might see 30 conversions in a week. In the final analysis, both may be found to be equally faithful in the exercise of their gift.

Variations and degrees, as the gifts themselves, are distributed at the discretion of God. Just as the master in the parable of the talents gave to one five talents, to another two and to yet another one (see Matt. 25:15), so God in His wisdom gives to each of us "a measure of faith" (Rom. 12:3). This is why, when gifts are in operation properly, Christians who have different degrees of the same gift have no cause for jealousy or envy. My left hand is not envious of my right hand because it may not be able to develop skills equal to my right hand. Rather, the two hands work together harmoniously for the benefit of the whole body. For example, God has given me a gift of teaching, but I want to teach as well as John Maxwell when I grow up! Until then, I'm happy using the talents that God has chosen to give me.

CHURCHES HAVE GIFT-MIXES, TOO

The philosophy of ministry of many local churches and that of certain denominations includes a particular position on spiritual gifts. One of the most frequent is the teaching called cessationism, which argues that certain gifts, called sign gifts, ceased with the age of the apostles. I have traced some of the history of this cessationist theory in chapter 1, so here I need only to stress that it remains an ongoing point of debate today.

I am impressed that both sides of the sign-gifts issue have such wonderful Christian leaders. Merrill Unger argues that the sign gifts of healing, working of miracles, tongues, interpretation, word of knowledge, prophecy and apostle are no longer needed in our churches.[20] John Walvoord's list of gifts that have passed away includes apostleship, prophecy, miracles, healing, tongues, interpretation and discerning of spirits.[21] John Stott would exclude apostles, prophets and possibly workers of miracles.[22] John MacArthur feels that the temporary gifts include miracles, healing, tongues and interpretation.[23]

Authors who take the contrary position, namely that the gifts mentioned above are in operation today, include an equally impressive list of blue-chip leaders. Among them are Leslie Flynn, B. E. Underwood, Donald Gee, Rick Yohn, Kenneth Kinghorn, Charles Hummel and others. Michael Griffiths argues the point strongly and even hints that the dispensational cessationist position is uncomfortably close to being a form of liberalism.[24] The most sustained and convincing refutation of the cessationist position is Jack Deere's *Surprised by the Power of the Spirit.*[25]

Some leaders have been on both sides of the sign-gifts controversy. Earl Radmacher, president emeritus of Western Baptist Seminary in Portland, Oregon, was raised in the Pentecostal tradition but has left it and now firmly opposes the use of tongues in the churches. Rodman Williams, a Presbyterian scholar who formerly took the Warfield view that miraculous gifts had ceased, became a faculty member of Regent University. A convinced charismatic, Williams says, "Now we wonder how we could have misread the New Testament for so long!"[26]

When I lived in Southern California, two of my favorite churches were located in the San Fernando Valley. I happened to visit one of them, Grace Community Church of the Valley, on a Sunday morning when Pastor John MacArthur was preaching the first message in a series entitled, "What Is Wrong with the Charismatic Movement?" On another Sunday, I happened to visit The Church On The Way and heard Pastor Jack Hayford give a message in tongues and interpret it right in the worship service. Both churches were growing at phenomenal rates. One had a Sunday attendance of 9,000, the other 8,000. Both had members who dearly loved Jesus Christ, who wanted to serve Him and who were growing in their faith. Both believed in and practiced spiritual gifts. God had blessed them both. Yet they disagreed about which of the gifts ought to be in use in churches today.

My studies of the growing churches in America have led me to believe that the question of which spiritual gifts may or may not now be in effect is not a primary growth factor across the board. Much more important seems to be the recognition that the Holy Spirit is working through spiritual gifts and that Christians need to discover, develop and use the ones that they believe are in effect to do the ministry of the Church.

How is all this explained then? My own conclusion is that, just as God gives specific gift-mixes to various people, He may also give specific gift-mixes to various churches and denominations. The gift-mix of a church or denomination should rightly be one of the determining factors of its philosophy of ministry. Churches that have varying philosophies of ministry are a part of the beautiful variety that God has built into the universal Body of Christ. Because people are different from one another, churches also need to be different from each other—if they are going to win unbelievers to Christ and fold them into responsible membership. I would not be inclined to suggest that the philosophy of ministry of either Grace Community Church or The Church On The Way should necessarily change. In my opinion, God loves them equally, and His blessing on both has been evident.

As far as church growth is concerned, establishing a firm philosophy of ministry should be a high priority. Each church needs to be able to articulate just what it stands for and what makes it different from other churches in the area. This is a sign of strength. The less frequently a philosophy of ministry is revised, the more the potential for growth is possible for the church.

REFLECTIONS

1. When a person is ordained to Christian ministry, it should be presumed that he or she has the appropriate spiritual gift or gifts for that particular ministry. But such is not always the case. Why? Can you give any examples?
2. What is the general attitude of the people in your

church regarding single adults? How would recognition of the gift of celibacy affect that attitude?

3. Discuss the implications of the principle that every person with a given spiritual gift is part of a ministry in the Body of Christ.

4. Some students of spiritual gifts conclude that certain gifts are in operation today that are not mentioned specifically as gifts in the Bible. Do you agree? Why or why not?

5. Do you think anyone you know might have the gift of intercession? Is this person aware that intercession may be a spiritual gift?

Notes

1. Laurence J. Peter and Raymond Hull, *The Peter Principle* (New York: Bantam Books, 1969), p. 7.
2. Festo Kivengere, *I Love Idi Amin* (Grand Rapids, MI: Fleming H. Revell Co., 1977).
3. Jean Dye Johnson, *God Planted Five Seeds* (New York: HarperCollins Publishers, 1966).
4. I told this story briefly in the preface to the first edition of *Defeat of the Bird God* (Grand Rapids, MI: Zondervan Publishing House, 1967), but the preface was not reprinted when the William Carey Library edition was printed later.
5. David B. Barrett and Todd M. Johnson, eds., *World Christian Trends A.D. 30-A.D. 2200* (Pasadena, CA: William Carey Library, 2001), p. 229.
6. For the core of this definition, I am indebted to Leslie B. Flynn, *Nineteen Gifts of the Spirit* (Wheaton, IL: Victor Books, 1974), p. 10.
7. Karen Mains, *Open Heart, Open Home* (Elgin, IL: David C. Cook Publishing, 1976).
8. Karen Mains, "Hospitality Means More Than a Party," *Moody* (December 1976), p. 38; another article on Karen Mains was written by Ron Wilson, "Open Hearted Living," *Christian Life* (July 1976), p. 26.
9. Edith Schaeffer, "Hospitality: Optional or Commanded?" *Christianity Today* (December 17, 1976), pp. 28-29.
10. A careful study of the use of hospitality by early Christians was done by

Donald Wayne Riddle, "Early Christian Hospitality: A Factor in the Gospel Transmission," *Journal of Biblical Literature* 57 (1938), pp. 141-154.

11. Elizabeth O'Connor, *Eighth Day of Creation: Gifts and Creativity* (Dallas: Word Books, 1971), p. 32.

12. Bryan Pollock, "Have You Ever Tried to Pray (for Eight Hours a Day)?" *Worldwide Challenge* (January 1978), pp. 12-14.

13. Norman Grubb, *Rees Howells: Intercessor* (Fort Washington, PA: Christian Literature Crusade, 1973), p. 86.

14. C. Peter Wagner, *Prayer Shield* (Ventura, CA: Regal Books, 1992), p. 49.

15. Robert Andrescik, "An Audience of One: An Interview with Ron Kenoly," *Ministries Today* (March/April 2004), p. 17.

16. Tim Hughes, *Here I Am to Worship* (Ventura, CA: Regal Books, 2004), pp. 62-63.

17. Ibid., p. 67.

18. William J. McRae, *The Dynamics of Spiritual Gifts* (Grand Rapids, MI: Zondervan Publishing House, 1976), p. 59.

19. Ray C. Stedman, *Body Life* (Ventura, CA: Regal Books, 1972), pp. 40-41.

20. Merrill F. Unger, *The Baptism and Gifts of the Holy Spirit* (Chicago, IL: Moody Press, 1974), p. 139.

21. John F. Walvoord, *The Holy Spirit* (Grand Rapids, MI: Zondervan Publishing House, 1954), pp. 173-188.

22. John R. W. Stott, *One People* (Downers Grove, IL: InterVarsity Press, 1968), p. 27; see also John R. W. Stott, *Baptism and Fullness: The Work of the Holy Spirit Today* (Downers Grove, IL: InterVarsity Press, 1976), pp. 94-102.

23. John MacArthur, Jr., *The Church, the Body of Christ* (Grand Rapids, MI: Zondervan Publishing House, 1973), p. 150.

24. Michael Griffiths, *Cinderella's Betrothal Gifts* (Robesonia, PA: OMF Books, 1978), p. 8.

25. Jack Deere, *Surprised by the Power of the Spirit* (Grand Rapids, MI: Zondervan Publishing House, 1993).

26. J. Rodman Williams, *The Era of the Spirit* (Plainfield, NJ: Logos International, 1971), p. 28.

Chapter 4

FOUR THINGS
THAT GIFTS ARE NOT

Paul says, "Now concerning spiritual gifts, brethren, I do not want you to be ignorant" (1 Cor. 12:1).

As an important step toward dispelling ignorance about spiritual gifts, we must be sure that confusion in some key areas does not throw people off the track. In my experience, I have come across four of these areas that need special attention. Spiritual gifts are often confused with (1) natural talents; (2) the fruit of the Spirit; (3) Christian roles; and, to some extent, (4) counterfeit gifts.

Let's look at these key areas one at a time.

DON'T CONFUSE SPIRITUAL GIFTS WITH NATURAL TALENTS

Every human being, by virtue of being made in the image of God, possesses certain natural talents. As with spiritual gifts, the natural talents have different variations and degrees. Talents are one of the features that give every human being a unique personality. Part of our self-identity is wrapped up in the particular mix of talents we have.

Where do these natural talents come from? Ultimately, they

are given by God, and as such they should be recognized in a broad sense as gifts. That is why we often say of a person who sings well or who has an extraordinary IQ or who can hit a golf ball into a hole from a long distance, "My, isn't that person gifted?"

Atheists Have Natural Talents

Having natural talents has nothing directly to do with being a Christian or being a member of the Body of Christ. Many atheists, for example, have superb talents for one thing or another. They have natural talents, but they do not have spiritual gifts. And the ultimate source of these talents, of course, is God our creator.

Christians, like anyone else, also have natural talents. But natural talents should not be confused with spiritual gifts. It is technically incorrect for a Christian to say that his or her "gift" is repairing automobiles or gourmet cooking or telling jokes or painting pictures or playing basketball. Those are all natural talents.

To make matters worse, the biblical word "charisma" has been secularized. I understand that in Greek literature the apostle Paul is the only known author who uses "charisma" frequently. The only other known appearances of "charisma," I understand from the scholars, are in 1 Peter 4:10 and once in Philo's writings. But a century ago, a famous German sociologist, Max Weber, began to use the Greek word "charisma" to describe a certain kind of leader, whom he called a charismatic leader. In that sense, the word is now used in secular circles of an Osama bin Laden or a Fidel Castro or a Saddam Hussein, to name a few international figures who have been recognized as charismatic, in the broad sense of the word. But none of the three, as far as I know, would have considered himself a member of the Body of Christ, and thus none of them has been given a spiritual gift.

Spiritual gifts are reserved exclusively for Christians. No unbeliever has one, and every true believer in Jesus does. Spiritual gifts are not to be regarded as dedicated natural talents. The two may have a discernible relationship, however, because in many cases (not all, by any means) God will choose to take the natural talent in an unbeliever and transform it into a spiritual gift when that person enters the Body of Christ. But in such a case, the spiritual gift is more than just a souped-up natural talent. Because it is only given by God, a spiritual gift can never be cloned.

Consider, for example, the natural talent of teaching. A significant segment of the population are teachers by profession. But, as most every pastor knows, not every well-trained, competent public school teacher also turns out to be a good Sunday School teacher. Why? In such cases, God evidently did not choose to transform the *talent* of teaching into the *gift* of teaching. But in many other cases, He does that very thing, and certain schoolteachers are also excellent Sunday School teachers.

DON'T CONFUSE SPIRITUAL GIFTS WITH THE FRUIT OF THE SPIRIT

The fruit of the Spirit is described in Galatians 5:22-23. Such things as love, joy, peace, longsuffering, kindness, goodness, faithfulness, gentleness and self-control are listed there. Some Bible expositors point out that "fruit" is in the singular, and that the original Greek construction would permit a colon after love. So although all these other things are part of the fruit, love could well be the primary one.

It is improper to speak of the gift of love, if by "gift" we mean that love should be seen as spiritual gift number 29 on our list. In the broad sense, of course, love is a gift from God and should be so regarded. "We love Him [God] because He first loved us" (1 John 4:19). But love is not a charisma in the sense that God gives it to some members of the Body, but not to others.

The Fruit Is for All

The fruit of the Spirit is the normal, expected outcome of Christian growth, maturity, holiness, Christlikeness and fullness of the Holy Spirit. Because all Christians have the responsibility of growing in their faith, all have the responsibility of developing the fruit of the Spirit. Fruit is not *discovered* as are the gifts; it is *developed* through the believer's walk with God and through yieldedness to the Holy Spirit. Although spiritual gifts help define what a Christian *does*, the fruit of the Spirit helps define what a Christian *is*.

The fruit of the Spirit is the indispensable foundation for the effective exercise of spiritual gifts. Gifts without fruit are worthless. The Corinthian believers found this out the hard way. They had an ideal gift-mix, according to 1 Corinthians 1:7. They were busy discovering, developing and using their spiritual gifts. They were as charismatic as a church can get. Yet they were a spiritual disaster area, one of the most messed up churches we read about in the New Testament.

Their basic problem was not gifts; it was fruit. That is why Paul wrote 1 Corinthians 13 to them. In it, he waxed eloquent about love, the fruit of the Spirit. He told them they could have the gift of tongues, the gift of prophecy, the gift of knowledge, the gift of faith, the gift of voluntary poverty, the gift of martyrdom and any other gift, but without love they amounted to absolutely nothing (see 1 Cor. 13:1-3). Gifts without fruit are like automobile tires without air—the ingredients are all there, but they are worthless.

Also, gifts are temporal, but fruit is eternal. In 1 Corinthians 13, we are also told that gifts such as prophecy, tongues and knowledge will vanish away. But faith, hope and love—fruit—will abide. Whereas gifts are task-oriented, fruit is God-oriented.

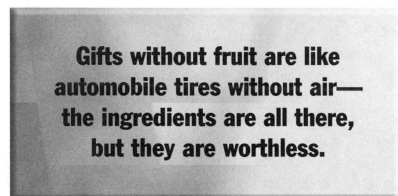

Gifts without fruit are like automobile tires without air— the ingredients are all there, but they are worthless.

It is worth noting that a passage on fruit accompanies every one of the primary passages on gifts. First Corinthians 13 is the most explicit and most widely recognized, which follows 1 Corinthians 12, where the gifts are featured. But also, the list of gifts ending in Romans 12:8 is immediately followed by "let love be without hypocrisy" and "be kindly affectionate to one another with brotherly love" (vv. 9-10). The passage continues for another 11 verses. Then in Ephesians 4, the gifts passage ends with verse 16 and the fruit passage picks up in the next verse and carries through to chapter 5. Among other things, it says, "Walk in love, as Christ also has loved us" (v. 2). The passage on spiritual gifts beginning with 1 Peter 4:9 is immediately preceded with "above all things have fervent love for one another, for love will cover a multitude of sins" (v. 8).

DON'T CONFUSE SPIRITUAL GIFTS WITH CHRISTIAN ROLES

When we look at the list of 28 gifts, it becomes obvious that many of them describe activities expected of every Christian. At this point, it is helpful to distinguish between *spiritual gifts* and *Christian roles*. Roles are slightly different from the fruit of the Spirit in that they involve more doing than being. But they are similar to the fruit of the Spirit in that they are expected of every Christian.

Perhaps the most obvious spiritual gift that is also a Christian role would be faith. Becoming a Christian and first entering into the Body of Christ requires faith. And this faith, according to the Bible, is a gift of God (see Eph. 2:8-9). We are also told that faith is a part of the fruit of the Spirit (see Gal. 5:22) and that "without faith it is impossible to please [God]" (Heb. 11:6). In other words, the lifestyle of every Christian, without exception, is to be characterized by 24/7 faith. Over and above this, however, the spiritual gift of faith is given by God to relatively few members of the Body. This will be described in some detail later on. But the *gift* of faith is much more than the *fruit* of faith or the *role* of faith, both of which we expect to see in every committed Christian.

For example, while discussing the gift of hospitality in the last chapter, I mentioned that neither Doris nor I has that particular gift. However, we do have a *role* of entertaining guests, and we do it with some regularity. Having people over for dinner, occasionally putting up a person for the night, taking a visitor on an outing, hosting church parties, loaning our car, making sure that new people are oriented to the community and things like that are all included in our Christian role. None of these things comes easily to us, and we probably do not do it as often or as well as we should, but we do make an effort because we feel that offering hospitality is simply part of being a good Christian.

Prayer is another example of a Christian role. It is both a privilege and a responsibility of every Christian. One does not need the gift of intercession to talk to God or to stand in the gap. Likewise, some Christians have the spiritual gift of serving, but all Christians should take seriously their role of serving one another (see Gal. 5:13). Some have the spiritual gift of exhortation, but all have a general role of exhorting one another (see Heb. 10:25). Only a few have the gift of evangelist, but all Christians are expected to exercise their role of witness (see Acts 1:8).

The Role of Celibacy

The role of celibacy is an important one to stress in our contemporary, permissive society when some people are trying to establish a "new morality." In the discussion of the gift of celibacy (see chapter 3), I indicated that I do not have the gift and that I have worked this out in a godly way by marrying a wife. But I do have a *role* of celibacy, which I particularly need to exercise when I am traveling away from home. Opportunities for unfaithfulness are usually not lacking if one is looking for them. I recall one unusual occasion in a rural hotel in Taiwan where, without my knowledge, the hotel manager had, as a matter of routine, already assigned a female sleeping partner to my room. I must admit that when I took a look at her, no real temptation was involved, but it certainly could have been. And even if she had looked like Miss Taiwan, I would still have been responsible to God to exercise my role of celibacy.

By the same token, the role of celibacy is apropos to Christians who have not yet married and to men and women who have lost a spouse through death or divorce. Most of the latter have already discovered that they do not have the gift of celibacy, and yet they need to find a way to be a Christian widow or divorcee and maintain continence until God provides another partner. Not having the gift of celibacy is no excuse for extramarital sex at any time.

Use Roles Whenever Necessary

Christians need to be ready to exercise any role in case of emergency or need. You may not be a doctor, but when an accident occurs, you help the victim as much as you can until the doctor arrives. When a fire starts, you extinguish what flames you can until the trained firefighters arrive. Many Christians are spared situations such as these in their spiritual lives, but some, pastors of churches for example, find themselves having to minister from roles—rather than gifts—a good bit of the time simply because the needs are there and someone has to take care of them whether they have special gifts or not.

Once, when I spoke at a church about spiritual gifts, in my presentation I mentioned that gifts are distributed in the Body of Christ much like assignments are distributed on a football team. I mentioned that offensive guards or tackles do not make touchdowns and get their names in the headlines, but without guards and tackles, the team would lose, because the running backs then could not make touchdowns either. After the meeting, a big man came up to me and told me that he had played offensive tackle in college. I asked him if he had ever made a touchdown. He smiled a broad smile and said he had made one once. It was a freak play. When the ball popped out of the runner's arms, he stopped blocking, grabbed the ball in the air and started running—and he became one of the few tackles in the NCAA ever to make a touchdown. His gift, in this analogy, was blocking; but in running the ball for a touchdown, he was exercising a role, just as Christians should when such opportunities arise.

The way Christian roles operate alongside spiritual gifts is vividly illustrated by the gift of giving.

THE GIFT OF GIVING

Every Christian is supposed to give part of his or her income to the Lord. According to the Bible, every believer should set definite, personal giving goals and give cheerfully (see 2 Cor. 9:7). This is a Christian role, and no exceptions are allowed that I am aware of. Rich Christians should give, and poor Christians should give. Young marrieds who have low incomes and high expenses should give alongside more mature empty nesters who are financially secure. New Christians should be taught to give as soon as they begin growing in their faith.

How much should believers give?

Ten Percent Is a Minimum

As I read the Scriptures, I think it is plain that a tithe, meaning 10 percent of one's income off the top, is the bare minimum for exercising the role of giving. I am not ordinarily legalistic in my views of Christian behavior, but I believe anyone who is under the 10 percent figure is engaging in a form of spiritual cheating. Some cheat the IRS regularly and get away with it. No one cheats God and gets away with it. "Do not be deceived, God is not mocked; for whatever a man sows, that he will also reap" (Gal. 6:7).

A sad but well-known fact is that a large number of Christians are not exercising their role of giving. In 1992, the average giving for Christians in America was something around $335 per year. The average salary, quite obviously, was considerably more than $3,350! The church I was attending at the time,

Lake Avenue Church in Pasadena, California, was a fairly affluent church, basically upper-middle class. However, I once figured
that if all our members were to receive only California welfare
payments and were to tithe, our income would go up by 40 percent! In 1999, seven years later, the average giving of Christians
to nonprofit organizations and churches had not increased. In
fact, it decreased to $300 per year.[1]

The Graduated Tithe

I began taking the role of giving seriously when, back in the
1970s, our pastor, Raymond Ortlund, preached a memorable
stewardship sermon during our November fund-raising drive.
Among other things, he told us that he and his wife gave 25
percent of their income off the top. My wife and I did some cal-
culating and found that we were barely over the minimal 10
percent. So we prayed and decided to raise our giving by one or
two percentage points a year until we reached 15 percent. Then
we would pray again. During the process, we discovered that
God's promise, "Give, and it will be given to you: good measure, pressed down, shaken together, and running over" (Luke
6:38), is literally true. We passed the 15 percent mark long ago,
and we have practiced the "graduated tithe" ever since. Each
year that our income goes up, our percentage of giving also
goes up.

For years, I denied that I had the gift of giving. But to be
honest, God has blessed my wife and me with higher annual
incomes for so many years that the percentage we now give is
admittedly far out of the range of most committed believers. Ray
Ortlund's sermon set us on a pathway that allowed us, over a
period of time, to discover a spiritual gift that otherwise might
have remained dormant.

LeTourneau and Tam

R. G. LeTourneau, the great Texas industrialist, was known for his gift of giving. He wrote, "The question is not how much of my money I give to God, but rather how much of God's money I keep."[2] He answered this question for himself by turning 90 percent of the assets of his company over to his Christian foundation, and then he and his wife gave in cash 90 percent of the income that was realized from the share of the business he kept. He and his wife never lacked any material things.

A more contemporary Christian brother with the gift of giving is Stanley Tam, who is in the silver business in Lima, Ohio. He made God the senior partner of his business by legally turning 51 percent over to his Christian foundation and then raising it over a period of time to 100 percent. The foundation receives the profits from the business. It almost goes without saying that he and his wife tithe their own family income as well. Without using the exact words, Stanley Tam recognizes his unusual ability to give to the Lord as a spiritual gift. He makes a point of avoiding the temptation of gift projection. He says in his autobiography, "I frankly don't believe I'm as good a businessman as our financial statements indicate. I believe I operate far above my natural capacity."[3] In another place he is careful to say, "Let me urge you not to use me as an example. . . . God has made what might be called singular demands on my life. He may do the same to you or choose to orient and motivate you in completely different ways."[4]

Although such highly successful people as LeTourneau and Tam are usually the ones recognized and given as examples in books such as this, the gift of giving is given to lower-income people as well. The apostle Paul mentions the Christians in Macedonia who gave out of their poverty (see 2 Cor. 8:1-2). Jesus' comment that the widow's mite was more than what the rich people gave is well known (see Mark 12:41-44). James McCormick, who owns a construction business in Birmingham, Alabama, is now a millionaire. But he discovered his gift of giving while he was working in a clothing store and earning $35 a week. At that time he made a promise to give 50 percent of his income to the Lord and has been doing so ever since. There is no question that the $17.50 a week he gave then was worth just as much to God as the very sizable amounts that he is now able to give.[5]

> *The gift of giving is the special ability God gives to certain members of the Body of Christ to contribute their material resources to the work of the Lord liberally and cheerfully, above and beyond the tithes and offerings expected of all believers.*

THE GIFT OF VOLUNTARY POVERTY

I am indebted to Donald Bridge and David Phypers for bringing the gift of voluntary poverty to my attention.[6] The biblical reference is 1 Corinthians 13:3, a passage in which Paul is contrasting spiritual gifts with the fruit of the Spirit (e.g., love). It says, "Though I bestow all my goods to feed the poor." For years, I simply assumed this was another way of describing the gift of giving, but now I understand that it is different, although often related. I would think that everyone who has the gift of voluntary poverty also has the gift of giving. However, not all who have the gift of giving have the corresponding gift of voluntary poverty.

> *The gift of voluntary poverty is the special ability that God gives to certain members of the Body of Christ to renounce material comfort and luxury and adopt a personal lifestyle equivalent to those living at the poverty level in a given society in order to serve God more effectively.*

The use of the adjective "voluntary" is important here to separate those with the gift of poverty from those who find themselves poverty stricken because of uncontrollable social circumstances. Furthermore, it must be recognized that wealth and poverty are only relative terms. Poor, yes, but compared to what? When we first began to think through the implications of this gift, Doris and I wondered if we might have had the gift of poverty when we were missionaries in Bolivia. After all, in 1971, the last year we were on the mission field, the total income for our family of five was $3,900. If we had earned this income in America's 1971 economy, we certainly would have considered ourselves poor. But while in Bolivia, we were able to live considerably above the poverty level on that kind of budget. We had to admit we did not have the gift.

Wesley and Müller

John Wesley, however, did have the hyphenated gift of giving-voluntary poverty. When he died, he left a well-worn frock coat and two silver teaspoons in his estate. But during his lifetime he had given $150,000 to the Lord.[7]

George Müller of Bristol was another man who had the gift of giving-voluntary poverty. He died having a total personal estate of $850. He lived as a poor man all his life. Yet when his books were audited after his death, it was discovered—much to everyone's surprise—that through the years a donor identified only as "a servant of the Lord Jesus, who, constrained by the love of Christ, seeks to lay up treasure in heaven" had given a total of $180,000. The donor of course was Mr. Müller himself.[8]

John Wesley and George Müller stand in contrast to R. G. LeTourneau and Stanley Tam, who illustrate the gift of giving *without* the gift of voluntary poverty. I appreciate Stanley Tam's candid statement, "I like good food, a comfortable house, decent clothes, a good car."[9] Most likely, God has called Tam to be rich instead of poor so that he can better exercise the gift of giving. Tam frankly says, "I have an insatiable thirst to make money. I love it. I like to promote, to see the company grow. I study our yearly and interim reports like a hungry hawk, evaluating, discovering, making checks and counterchecks."[10]

People's Christian Coalition

Such an attitude is out of keeping with the kind of activity being done by another group of American Christians who call themselves the People's Christian Coalition. They exercise their gift of voluntary poverty by choosing to live a simple lifestyle in a commune in the poor section of Washington, D.C. They are doing a wonderful thing in using their gifts to contribute to the well-being of the poor and oppressed in Washington's ghetto. The public statements published in their magazine, *Sojourners*, however, may approach the syndrome of gift projection. They spend a good deal of time attempting to produce biblical reasons why the kind of radical lifestyle they have developed might be more pleasing to God than the lifestyle of other Christians in our society who have and are exercising other spiritual gifts but who are living at a more affluent economic level. They associate people who choose not to imitate them with the so-called establishment, which is then blamed for a variety of social and economic evils.

Perhaps this critical attitude is because of the presence of another gift—prophecy. Writings in *Sojourners* have a ring of pessimism reminiscent of Jeremiah or other Old Testament prophets. Because of their gift-mix, these radical evangelicals would probably feel as uncomfortable living in Billy Graham's

secluded estate on Black Mountain in North Carolina or in
Robert Schuller's commodious home in Orange, California, as
Billy Graham or Robert Schuller would feel living in a commune
in Washington's ghetto.

But "the eye cannot say to the hand, 'I have no need of you' "
(1 Cor. 12:21). Neither can nor should any members of the Body
having one gift-mix stand in harsh judgment of other members
of the Body who have another gift-mix. Perhaps, however, those
with a certain variety of the gift of prophecy feel they cannot do
otherwise and they need to be understood in that light by those
of the establishment.

Well-spent money can be a tremendous stimulus to church
growth. Much potential extension of the kingdom of God both
here in America and among the unreached peoples of the world
is currently hindered because of the lack of funds. I hope that
with the growing interest in spiritual gifts, thousands of believers will discover that God has given them the gift of giving and
millions who are not even exercising their Christian role of giving a tithe will start doing so responsibly. The resources subsequently released for the spread of the gospel and the care of the
suffering and oppressed would be awesome. God, I believe,
would be highly pleased.

DON'T CONFUSE SPIRITUAL GIFTS
WITH COUNTERFEIT GIFTS

I wish I did not have to write this section on counterfeit gifts. I
wish it were not true that Satan and his demons and evil spirits
are real and actively opposing the work of the Lord. Jesus
Himself said, "For false christs and false prophets will rise and
show great signs and wonders to deceive, if possible, even the
elect" (Matt. 24:24). Jesus also spoke about those who prophesy

and cast out demons in His name, but who, in reality, turn out to be workers of iniquity (see Matt. 7:22-23).

I do not doubt that Satan can and does counterfeit every gift on the list. He is a supernatural being and he has supernatural powers. His power was shown in a spectacular way in Egypt when Pharaoh's magicians could publicly match some of the works that God did through Moses (see Exod. 7—8). Of course, Satan's power is limited and controlled. I like the way Robert Tuttle puts it: "Satan is on a tether. If, however, we slip within reach or range of his tether, yielding to some particular temptation, he'll have us for breakfast."[11]

Raphael Gasson, now a Christian but formerly a spiritualist medium, wrote a rather chilling book on this subject, called *The Challenging Counterfeit*. He tells it like it is. I made the mistake of discussing the subject at the supper table one night and ruined my daughter Becky's appetite. Gasson's experience has shown him, "It is very obvious that Satan is using an extremely subtle counterfeit to the precious gifts of the Spirit."[12] In his book, Gasson describes several of Satan's counterfeits.

Gasson specifically shows, for example, how false gifts of faith, miracles, healing, tongues and interpretation of tongues are produced by Satan. The counterfeit of the gift of discerning spirits, he feels, is clairvoyance and clairaudience. The gift of deliverance is cleverly reproduced by the devil as well, and this is one of the reasons I no longer like to refer to it as the gift of exorcism.

Gasson recalls how Satan gave him the ability to prophesy, and he points out that most of these counterfeit prophecies came true. This is one way the devil makes his appeals more attractive. On one occasion during the war years, for example, a man brought to Gasson an item belonging to the man's son, who was in the service. The man wanted to find out where his son was. Through his "spirit guide" (who purported to be the spirit of an African witch doctor), Gasson found out that the owner of the item was well and a prisoner of war. The father then proceeded to show Gasson a telegram from the War Department stating that his son had been killed in action more than two weeks previously. Gasson went back to his guide and verified that the soldier-son really was not dead and that the father would have this confirmed in three days. Sure enough, three days later the father received a telegram from the War Department apologizing for the mistake and saying that the boy was well and a prisoner of war.[13]

Some naively interpret this kind of prophecy as a work of God. It is in reality the work of the devil. But it is no less real.

We immediately need to remind ourselves that God knows all about this deceitfulness and gives adequate power to His children to prevent it. For example, one of my colleagues on the Lausanne Committee for World Evangelization was Petrus Octavianus of Indonesia. On one occasion, he was speaking to an audience of 3,000 people in Stuttgart, Germany. At the end of his presentation, he asked for a time of silent prayer. When all was quiet, one man on the platform got up and began praying in tongues. Petrus Octavianus turned to him and in the name of Jesus commanded him to be silent. Octavianus later explained, "After I had prayed for clarity, it became clear to me that this speaking in tongues was not brought about by the Holy Spirit but by the enemy."[14]

I do not know if God has given Petrus Octavianus the gift of discerning of spirits, but if he does not have it, at that moment he would have been exercising one of those emergency Christian roles. It would be well at this point to take a brief look at the two spiritual gifts that most relate to this realm of darkness: discerning of spirits and deliverance.

THE GIFT OF
DISCERNING OF SPIRITS

The New Testament clearly teaches that every Christian needs to be able to distinguish good from evil, right from wrong. Hebrews 5:14 says that mature Christians "have their senses exercised to discern both good and evil." The Berean Christians were commended for not being naive. They tested the preaching of the apostles against Scripture, as we all must (see Acts 17:11). First John 4:1 is explicit in telling us to "not believe every spirit, but test the spirits, whether they are of God."

These passages describe the Christian role of discernment. Over and above what is expected of all Christians, however, is a spiritual gift of discerning of spirits given to relatively few. This gift may not be exercised frequently. Some who have it may be reluctant to use it because it requires a good deal of courage. But it is comforting for the whole Body to know that God has not left Christians ignorant or defenseless against the tactics of Satan and his forces of evil.

> *The gift of discerning (or discernment) of spirits is the special ability that God gives to certain members of the Body of Christ to know with assurance whether certain behaviors purported to be of God are in reality divine, human or satanic.*

The apostle Peter apparently had the gift of discerning of spirits. He used it dramatically when he discerned that Satan had inspired Ananias to lie about his real-estate deal, and Ananias was struck dead on the spot. He repeated it with Ananias's wife, Sapphira, who also died (see Acts 5:1-10). Later on in Samaria, Peter used the gift to see through to the heart motives of Simon the sorcerer. He had all the assurance from God that he needed in order to tell Simon that he was "poisoned by bitterness and bound by iniquity" (8:23).

The gift of discernment can operate on several levels. The most obvious being the ability to know that purportedly good behavior is in reality the work of Satan. This is the level on which Petrus Octavianus was ministering in Stuttgart. Another level is that of discerning whether something that a Christian brother or sister does is emerging from godly motives or carnal motives. A third level involves the supernatural ability to distinguish truth from error, although motives may be proper. It goes without saying that the latter two levels involve sensitive kinds of judgment and must be accompanied with an extra measure of the fruit of the Spirit if they are going to be helpful to the Body.

SPIRITUAL MAPPING

A further level for using the gift of discernment has opened in the field of spiritual mapping. Pioneered by George Otis, Jr., spiritual mapping is an attempt to see our world or our cities or any other human network as they *really are*, not as they *appear to be*. This means understanding, to the degree possible, both the redemptive purposes of God for a city or other human network and also the spiritual forces of darkness that are attempting to block God's purposes. Spiritual mapping is helping us to be more precise in our spiritual warfare.

Spiritual mappers who have the gift of discernment of spirits are enabled to see into the invisible world behind our visible surroundings. I am not one who has this gift, but several who do collaborated with me in the first instructional book on spiritual mapping, *Breaking Strongholds in Your City*. This has been a significant tool in advancing the cause of world evangelization, and I recommend it highly to those desiring more information.

THE GIFT OF
DELIVERANCE

Although the gift of deliverance, sometimes referred to as the gift of exorcism, is one of the gifts not mentioned in the Bible specifically as a charisma, abundant evidence shows that it was at work in the New Testament and that it is at work in our contemporary world.[15]

> *The gift of deliverance is the special ability that God gives to certain members of the Body of Christ to cast out demons and evil spirits.*

It is reasonable to believe that the combination of the gifts of discernment and deliverance is another of the hyphenated gifts such as pastor-teacher. They seemed to be operating together when the apostle Paul, for example, became annoyed with the young girl in Philippi who kept saying, "These men are the servants of the Most High God, who proclaim to us the way of salvation" (Acts 16:17). These words do not sound as though anything would be wrong with them. But Paul was able to discern that it was actually an evil spirit speaking through the girl, and he cast out the spirit (see v. 18).

A deliverance ministry will not be effective over the long haul without the discernment of spirits. At the same time, situations can and do arise when a demon will manifest unexpectedly and we have to step in, take authority and bind the spirit or cast it out, whether or not we have gifts of deliverance or discernment. This is our Christian role. Biblical Christians are sensitive to the demonic and they are prepared to deal with demons when necessary. I myself, for example, do not have the gift of deliverance, but I nevertheless have been used to cast out many demons over the years.

Varieties of Deliverance Ministries

Although I do not have the gift of deliverance, my wife, Doris, does, and she prays for demonized people as a part of her ongoing ministry. I know several others who have the gift and ministry of deliverance, and God seems to show them a variety of formats and methods. Some people counsel the demonized as "patients" over a period of time and charge fees. Some, such as Carlos Annacondia of Argentina, do mass deliverance. In his open-air evangelistic crusades, Annacondia erects a tent 150-feet long and calls it his spiritual intensive-care unit. It is not unusual for 200 or 300 people to be delivered from demons in one night. Others, such as my colleague Charles Kraft, combine ministries of inner healing with deliverance. Dr. Kraft explains his methods in detail in his excellent book *Defeating Dark Angels*. Some find it helpful to allow the demons to speak during deliverance, and others keep them silent.

Doris has yet another format. She schedules a two- to three-hour block of time for a deliverance session in her Global Harvest Ministries office. She often wishes she would receive "words of knowledge," or direct revelations from God, about the spirits causing a particular affliction. But since she ordinarily does not, she has developed an 11-page confidential questionnaire, which the demonized person must complete in full disclosure some days before the session. The evening before the appointment, Doris studies and prays over the questionnaire for 20 to 30 minutes. When she is finished, she knows fairly precisely what approach she will take the next day.

Doris fasts on the day of deliverance. Another person whom she is mentoring often accompanies her. Doris takes authority and forbids the evil spirits to speak or manifest in any way. Because her gift is deliverance and not exhortation, she does no traditional counseling. She does not schedule repeat appointments. With very few exceptions, the demonized person leaves totally freed from the affliction. Doris destroys the questionnaire, except for a legally binding release form the person has previously signed. Doris does not charge for her ministry, but the touching letters she receives from those who have been dramatically healed and whose lives have been transformed through the power of the Holy Spirit are reward enough.

Her approach to deliverance, including the questionnaire, is found in her book *How to Cast Out Demons*.

Deliverance and Evangelism

One of the most dramatic cause-and-effect relationships between deliverance and evangelism I am aware of began in Pasadena, California. A young man from Bolivia, Julio Cesar Ruibal, was studying premed at Pasadena City College. On the side, he happened to be the youngest and reportedly one of the two most powerful gurus of a certain branch of the occult in the whole Western Hemisphere. But God had His hand on the young man. Julio first heard the gospel in a Kathryn Kuhlman meeting and found himself very confused. The next day he attended a prayer meeting at the home of a couple from the church I was attending, Lake Avenue Church. Two ladies were there, both of whom had the gift of deliverance. In a spine-tingling testimony, Ruibal tells how he was delivered from the demons of yoga, clairvoyance, astrology, voodoo, reincarnation, the kabala, levitation, metaphysical healing, automatic writing, use of the pendulum, extrasensory perception and others. When the demons left, they cast him on the floor, and Julio says it felt like an electric current going out of his body.[16]

As Julio Cesar Ruibal grew in the Lord, he felt called to return to Bolivia to preach the gospel. By then he had discovered he had the gift of healing. The meetings he held in Bolivia in 1973 turned out to be the most spectacular evangelistic meetings in that country before or since.[17] Thousands of people who found the Lord through his ministry in Bolivia (including then President Banzer's wife) can thank the Lord also for the two ladies in Pasadena who had the gift of deliverance and who knew how to use it. Parenthetically, Julio Cesar later became a martyr when hoodlums in Colombia assassinated him for his faith.

HOW LONG DO YOU KEEP YOUR GIFT?

Do spiritual gifts come and go? I don't think so.

In my opinion, once a person is given a bona fide spiritual gift, it is a lifetime possession. This is derived from Romans 12:4, where Paul establishes the analogy of the physical body as the hermeneutical key for understanding spiritual gifts. If spiritual gifts are to the Body of Christ as hands, tongues and other members are to the physical body, I have little question in my mind that once we know what our gifts are, we can depend on keeping them. I do not go to bed at night having any worry whatsoever that tomorrow my foot might wake up a kidney. Both the development of a spiritual gift in the life of an individual Christian and the smooth operation of the Body of Christ as a whole depend on similar confidence.

Accountability

Knowing that we will keep our gifts and be accountable for what we do with them at the final judgment helps us to plan our lives. For one thing, it can keep us from expending excessive energy in using appealing Christian roles at the expense of energy that could be used for exercising our spiritual gifts. The health of a church depends on effectively mobilizing of all its members to minister. Research shows that the average active Christian layperson will give something between 3 to 10 hours a week to the church and to ministry. A 10-hour-a-week church member is a gem—most are much lower than that, and it is unrealistic to plan for much of anything different.

In many churches, most of the hours available are taken up with morning and evening worship services, Sunday School, prayer meetings and small group meetings. For the majority of people, this is a time for personal spiritual growth, not for ministry. The relatively little time left over for ministry should be carefully planned and structured. Activities that divert energy from ministry should be kept to a minimum.

My rule of thumb is this: Spiritual gifts should be used in planned and structured time, and Christian roles should be exercised casually. For example, I think Stanley Tam, who has the gift of giving, does well in spending a good amount of his time on financial affairs, figuring out how he can make more money for the Lord. It was not always like this, but I have now arrived at a point in life in which I spend most of my discretionary time in activities directly related to exercising my spiritual gifts. Bobby Clinton calls this point in life convergence.[18]

Dominant and Subordinate Gifts

Multigifted people may find that during certain periods of their ministry, some of their gifts will be dominant and others subordinate. Their ranking order might vary over the years as circumstances change. In my opinion, however, this does not mean that they have lost a gift along the way.

At the same time, some gifts may become dormant against

God's will. You may have a gift you are supposed to be using but are not. This seemed to be what Paul had in mind when he had to keep exhorting Timothy, "Do not neglect the gift" (1 Tim. 4:14) and "stir up the gift" (2 Tim. 1:6) and "do the work of an evangelist" (4:5), assuming with good reason that evangelist was one of Timothy's spiritual gifts. Allowing gifts to become dormant is one of the ways we are in danger of quenching the Spirit (see 1 Thess. 5:19), and that should be avoided at all costs.

To illustrate, I want to use a fable attributed to Charles Swindoll when he was pastoring the Evangelical Free Church of Fullerton, California:

> A group of animals decided to improve their general welfare by starting a school. The curriculum included swimming, running, climbing and flying. The duck, an excellent swimmer, was deficient in other areas, so he majored in climbing, running and flying, much to the detriment of his swimming. The rabbit, a superior runner, was forced to spend so much of his time in other classes that he soon lost much of his famed speed. The squirrel, who had been rated "A" as a climber dropped to a "C" because his instructors spent hours trying to teach him to swim and fly. And the eagle was disciplined for soaring to the treetop when he had been told to learn how to climb, even though flying was most natural for him.[19]

What more needs to be said? Growing churches, such as the Evangelical Free Church, understand the dynamic of spiritual gifts and plan their church programs to maximize their effectiveness. They have learned that it is counterproductive to chain people's energies in activities for which they are not gifted. They concentrate on people's strengths in order to give the Holy Spirit free rein. They know how to set priorities. And the church grows.

REFLECTIONS

1. If it is true that spiritual gifts are not just dedicated natural talents, what is the difference?
2. Why is love not to be thought of as a spiritual gift?
3. Name several of the spiritual gifts; then, for each one, discuss what the corresponding role might be and how it would differ from the gift.
4. Discuss the concept of the graduated tithe. Do you feel that your pastor should teach this to your congregation? Why or why not?
5. Do you know of anyone in your church or your community who has the gift of deliverance? How does he or she exercise this gift?

Notes

1. The Barna Group, "Evangelicals Are the Most Generous Givers, but Fewer than 10% of Born Again Christians Give 10% to Their Church," *The Barna Update*, April 5, 2000. http://www.barna.org/FlexPage.aspx?Page=Barna Update&BarnaUpdateID=52 (accessed December 3, 2004).
2. R. G. LeTourneau, *Mover of Men and Mountains* (Chicago: Moody Press, 1972), p. 280.
3. Stanley Tam, *God Owns My Business* (Dallas: Word Books, 1969), p. 62.
4. Ibid., p. 3.
5. Reported in *Straight from the Shoulder* (April-May 1976), p. 4.
6. Donald Bridge and David Phypers, *Spiritual Gifts and the Church* (Downers Grove, IL: InterVarsity Press, 1973), pp. 78-81.
7. Basil Miller, *George Muller: The Man of Faith* (Grand Rapids, MI: Zondervan Publishing House, 1941), pp. 126-127.
8. Ibid.
9. Tam, *God Owns My Business*, p. 50.
10. Ibid., p. 47.
11. Robert G. Tuttle, *The Partakers: Holy Spirit Power for Persevering Christians*

(Nashville, TN: Abingdon Press, 1974), p. 61.

12. Raphael Gasson, *The Challenging Counterfeit* (Plainfield, NJ: Logos Books, 1966), p. 90.

13. Ibid., pp. 105-106.

14. Kurt E. Koch, *Charismatic Gifts* (Quebec, Canada: Association for Christian Evangelism, 1975), pp. 42-43.

15. In the original edition of this book, I used "exorcism" instead of "deliverance." Since then, I have found that experts in this ministry do not like "exorcism," because it carries overtones of non-Christian approaches to the demonic. They uniformly prefer "deliverance."

16. Ruibal's detailed testimony can be found in Nicky Cruz, *Satan on the Loose* (Tarrytown, NY: Fleming H. Revell, 1973), pp. 134-143.

17. The Bolivia ministry of Ruibal was reported in *Christianity Today* (March 16, 1973), p. 40.

18. J. Robert Clinton, *The Making of a Leader* (Colorado Springs, CO: NavPress, 1988), pp. 32-33.

19. *Daily Bread* (September 1, 1976).

Chapter 5

HOW I FOUND MY GIFTS AND HOW YOU CAN FIND YOURS

Nowhere does the Bible deal specifically with finding gifts. Nowhere, for example, does Peter or Paul or James say, "And now, brethren, I would have you follow these steps to discover your spiritual gift." The lack of such a passage has convinced some people that discovering gifts is an improper pursuit for Christians. I discussed these arguments, pro and con, in chapter 2.

In my opinion, the lack of such specific instructions in the Bible should not be a deterrent to set forth practical, twenty-first century procedures for knowing and doing God's will. Nowhere does the Bible tell us how to draw up the constitution and bylaws for a local church or what membership requirements should be for a local church. Nowhere does the Bible tell us how to organize a missionary society or how to support missionaries. For centuries, theologians and Bible students have been trying to determine exactly when and how Christians should be baptized. Most Christians do not find such things like this new or unusual.

I am not intimidated. Neither are other authors of most books on spiritual gifts. Many of the available books include chapters such as this one on how to discover your gift.

As I read through a number of books on spiritual gifts, I

found that most authors are saying practically the same thing. Few authors will lift someone else's outline and use it, so each one develops new wording. But the procedure for finding gifts is surprisingly similar from author to author. This is comforting, because it does seem that a consensus has been emerging, which helps reduce confusion and increase effectiveness. In any case, we who find ourselves in the field of teaching spiritual gifts are much closer to agreement with each other on how to do it than those, for example, who are dealing with the issue of baptism.

I have been using the five steps—which I will describe here—for so many years that I do not know where they might have come from. I would like to imagine that they are mine, but I am old enough now to understand what Solomon meant when he said, "There is nothing new under the sun" (Eccles. 1:9). For the 40 plus years I have been using these five steps in classes and seminars, I can report that they actually help people discover their gifts. It has been gratifying to see the steps emerging in several other books and manuals, further confirming to me that they have proved useful at least to some people.

BE MINDFUL OF THE FOUR FUNDAMENTAL PREREQUISITES

Before beginning to take the actual steps toward finding your gift, four fundamental prerequisites need to characterize your life. Leave out any one of them, and you will have a difficult time discovering your gift.

First, you have to be a Christian. Spiritual gifts are given only to members of the Body of Christ. Unfortunately, not all church members in America are truly members of the Body of Christ. Almost all churches, some more than others, have members who are not committed to Jesus. They may attend with some regularity, put money in the offering plate, belong to some boards or committees as well as teach Sunday School. Still, they have never come into that personal relationship with the Savior that some people call being born again and others call commitment to Christ or being saved or converted. The term used is much less important than the personal relationship with Jesus Christ.

When I go into a church, I cannot just assume that everyone there is ready to hear a teaching on spiritual gifts. Some may need teaching on salvation first. If you have a question in your mind, ask yourself honestly whether you can say that you have become a new creature in Christ—that old things are passed away and that everything has become new (see 2 Cor. 5:17). If the answer is no, postpone trying to discover your spiritual gift. Seek help in finding Christ as your personal Savior and Lord. Pray sincerely to God and expect the Scripture to be fulfilled, "Seek, and you will find" (Matt. 7:7). Find a person who is a born-again Christian and ask for advice. The Bible says, "If you confess with your mouth the Lord Jesus and believe in your heart that God has raised Him from the dead, you will be saved" (Rom. 10:9). Do this before you look for spiritual gifts, because if you are not yet in the Body, you do not have a spiritual gift at all.

Second, you have to believe in spiritual gifts. I am almost certain that the reason most Christians who do not believe in spiritual gifts don't is because they have not been told about them in an understandable way. In my long teaching experience, I cannot recall any Christian who has seriously listened to teaching on spiritual gifts and not become convinced that they must have one or more. But despite the books, seminars, sermons and training courses now available, probably the majority of

American Christians still have only a minimal knowledge of spiritual gifts. In most cases, it is not their fault. I get shivers down my spine when I read James 3:1: "My brethren, let not many of you become teachers, knowing that we shall receive a stricter judgment." This is uncomfortable, because it rightly shifts the blame for ignorance of spiritual gifts to those of us who are responsible to teach the Word of God to others. It is not that the doctrine of spiritual gifts is some obscure or vague New Testament teaching, as are baptizing for the dead and determining the time of the rapture. Rather, it is one of the clearest teachings the Bible offers us.

This, then, becomes a question of faith. You must believe that God has given you a spiritual gift before you start the process of discovering it. In chapter 2, I try to inform all Christians who read this book that they do have spiritual gifts. If I have failed in your case, the five steps in this chapter may not be for you. For the steps to work, you must have a sense of gratitude to God that He has, in fact, given you a gift, and a sense of joyful anticipation in finding out what it is.

Third, you have to be willing to work. The five steps I am about to suggest constitute a spiritual exercise. God's help is needed to accomplish this. God has given you one or more spiritual gifts for a reason. He has a job He wants you to do in the Body of Christ, a specific job for which He has equipped you. God knows whether you are serious about working for Him. If He sees that you just want to discover your gift for the fun of it or because it is the in thing to do, you cannot expect Him to offer much help in doing it.

If, however, you promise to use your spiritual gift for the glory of God and for the welfare of the Body of Christ, He will help you. Recognize that this is God's best for you. Be open to what He wants to do through you. Discovering gifts is not an ego trip, although it will raise your self-esteem tremendously. If you are ready for a life as an active, productive Christian, you are ready for the five steps.

Fourth, you have to pray. Before, during and after this process you should pray. "If any of you lacks wisdom," James says, "let him ask of God, who gives to all liberally" (Jas. 1:5). Beseech God sincerely and earnestly for His guidance all the way through the five steps. Because God wants you to discover your spiritual gift, He certainly will give you all the help you need. Just ask and believe that He will. As you pray, listen to His voice. He will unlock the beautiful possibilities for the fruitful ministry He has already placed within you.

Knowing these four prerequisites, you are ready for the five steps necessary to discover your spiritual gift.

STEP 1: EXPLORE THE POSSIBILITIES

The first step in planning many human endeavors is to consider all the possible options. If you want to travel from Dallas to Philadelphia, for example, you need to know that it can be done by train, airplane, automobile, motorcycle, horseback, hitchhiking, bus and other ways. If you choose to drive, you look at a map and explore the various route possibilities. This is normal and logical.

It is difficult to discover a spiritual gift if you do not know approximately what to look for ahead of time. The purpose of this first step, exploring the possibilities, is to become familiar enough with the gifts that God ordinarily gives to the Body of Christ so that when you come across your gift later on, you will recognize it for what it really is.

Here are five ways to approach this exciting first step.

Study the Bible

Naturally, the basic source of data about the possible spiritual gifts is located in the Bible. Read the major passages on spiritual gifts time and again. Read them in several different versions. Find examples in the lives of good people in the Bible and how these gifts might have worked in practice. Using whatever helps are available, cross-check Scripture references until you feel you are familiar with what they reveal.

Learn Your Church's Position on Gifts

As I have mentioned several times, by no means is there universal agreement among churches and denominations about which gifts are in operation today. Nor would I expect these differences to be resolved in our generation.

Meanwhile, we have a generation of lost men and women who need to be won to Jesus Christ. We would be stupid to say that we will wait until we all agree on spiritual gifts to start evangelizing the world. No, let's go to it and evangelize the world by using the equipment God has given to us now. If the next generation will have better equipment or more consensus on one thing or another, that is of minor concern to us of this generation.

God is probably pleased with the variety of gift-mixes being used among the churches and denominations. We need to recognize that we are the way we are largely because God has made us that way. He gives some of His servants two talents and some five, but He expects us to use all of them to accomplish the master's purpose.

Because I believe strongly in commitment to the Body of Christ, I believe that when a person voluntarily joins a church, he or she ought to be under the discipline and authority of that church. On the matter of spiritual gifts, the major difference today usually surfaces over what we have referred to as the sign gifts—mainly speaking in tongues—but over others as well. Some churches expect the gift of tongues to be used in their worship services. Some have special services on a weekday when tongues are used, but they do not allow it in Sunday worship. Some do not allow tongues to be used at all at meetings held in the church, but they do not object to it in home cell groups or in private use, such as in private prayer. Other churches are convinced that tongues should not be used at all in our day and age.

Suppose you determine the position of your church on this and other gifts, but you disagree? I suggest one of two courses of action. Either decide to be loyal to your church and its belief, and practice without grumbling, or respectfully leave and ask God to take you to another church where you will feel more at home.

Notice, I do not recommend that you decide to stay where you are and try to convince the church or certain people in it to change their position. The energy such activity saps from the church is enormous. Many churches have gone through bitter splits over this issue because it has been allowed to fester under the surface until it could no longer be controlled. God did not give spiritual gifts for dissension and hard feelings. He gave spiritual gifts to enhance the health and vitality and growth of the Body. Every unit of spiritual energy being used to fight battles over spiritual gifts is one unit that cannot be used for ministry to the lost. I believe that God prefers our energies to be used in seeing that the lost are found and brought into the family of God.

As a church member, you have a right to know what your particular church believes about spiritual gifts. When you learn what it is, you will then have better parameters within which to take this first step of exploring the possibilities.

Read Extensively

Never before have Christian readers had available a richer literary fare on the subject of spiritual gifts. In this book, you will find my opinion as to what 28 of the spiritual gifts actually are, but it is by no means the last word. Read other books as well. List the points where authors agree on the definition of a particular gift and where they disagree. Put all that together with what you are learning from the Bible and formulate your own opinion. What difference does it really make if I think a gift is the gift of prophecy and someone else thinks it is the word of knowledge? God is overseeing the whole issue, and He is probably more broad-minded and more flexible than for what we give Him credit. In most cases, He can use us for His glory just the way we are.

Get to Know Gifted People

Seek out and talk to Christian people who have discovered and developed and are now using their spiritual gifts. Find out how they articulate what their gifts are and how they interpret their ministry through gifts.

Make Gifts a Conversation Piece

Christians today have come a long way in understanding spiritual gifts, but even so, a large number are still reluctant to talk about them to each other with ease. An attitude exists that says, "If I talk about my spiritual gift, people will think I am bragging" or "If I talk about not having a gift, it is a cop-out." I hope we will shed our inhibitions soon so that we will be able to share openly with each other what our gifts are and what they are not. This will help us and our friends and our children know what the optimum possibilities are for our ministry.

STEP 2: EXPERIMENT WITH AS MANY GIFTS AS YOU CAN

Ray Stedman wrote, "You discover a spiritual gift just like you discovered your natural talents!"[1]

You would never know you had a talent for bowling, for example, if you had not tried it. You would never know you could write poetry if you had never written some. I wonder if I have a talent for hang gliding? I will never know for sure unless I try it.

Obviously, some spiritual gifts on the list do not lend themselves easily to experimentation. I do not know how to suggest an experiment with the gift of martyrdom, for example. Although some gifts are like that, the majority are not. You can experiment with them, and I recommend you do as much experimenting as possible.

Looking for the Needs

A starting point is to look around and see what needs you can identify. Then try to do something to meet a need. Look for the needs of other people. Look for the needs of the church. Find out where you can be useful in any way, and do it.

Be available for any job around the church that you might be asked to do. When you get an assignment, undertake it in prayer. Ask the Lord to show you through that experience whether you might have a spiritual gift along those lines. Hang in there and work hard. Discovering gifts does not usually come quickly. Give each assignment a fair shake and do not give up easily.

Discovering Which Gifts You Do and Do Not Have

While you are experimenting with the gifts, it is just as important to answer the question, Which gifts *don't* I have? as it is to answer the opposite question, Which gifts *do* I have? Every gift that you find you do *not* have reduces the number of options you need to work at for getting the positive answer.

Let me tell a story that will highlight how important it is to discover, through experimenting, which gifts you do *not* have.

When I graduated from Fuller Seminary back in the mid-1950s, I had learned next to nothing about spiritual gifts. I think evangelical leaders by and large were still largely unsure of the Pentecostal movement at that time, and most had not yet articulated their own position on the gifts. In those days, we certainly were not taught that we had gifts and that we needed to discover, develop and use them. After seminary, an evangelical, Bible-believing church ordained me, but not one of the seven ministers on my ordaining council asked me if I had any spiritual gifts or if I happened to know what they were. I was accepted by and I served under two evangelical mission agencies. Neither one asked questions about my spiritual gifts on their application forms. So I went to Bolivia in 1956 being ignorant of spiritual gifts.

While I did not know much about spiritual gifts, I did know what I wanted to be. Those were the days when Billy Graham had just moved into orbit. He became the hero of many seminary students, including me. I marveled at the way he would preach to a stadium full of people, deliver a simple Bible message, give an invitation and see people get up all over the place, fill the aisles and pour down to the front to make a decision for Christ. That was for me! My friends and I would imitate Billy Graham's gestures in our preaching classes. We would try to preach with a North Carolina accent. We learned to declare "The Bible says . . ." and have appropriate sparks of fire in our eyes.

By the time I was ready to go to the mission field, I had it all figured out. Billy Graham could have America—I would take

Bolivia! In my mind, I could see thousands and thousands of Bolivians finding Christ through my messages.

I had to spend some time learning Spanish, of course, but when I did, I was ready to begin. I prepared a beautiful sermon in Spanish and used all the homiletical skills I had learned in seminary. I thought the sermon also had one or two things in it that Billy Graham himself might not have thought of. Then I preached the sermon with all my heart and gave the invitation. Nobody came!

Disappointed and somewhat dejected, I tried to figure out what had happened. Perhaps it had to do with prayer. Even at best I have never been a great prayer warrior, but with all the effort it took me to prepare the sermon that time, I had to admit that I had hardly prayed at all. So I prepared another sermon using symmetrical design and sound doctrine. But this time I prayed intensely before I went into the pulpit. The results were the same. People acted as if they were permanently glued to their seats.

I then thought something in my life must be blocking my relationship with the Lord. The consecration theology I was taught had programmed me to feel that I must properly be presenting my body as "a living sacrifice" (Rom. 12:1), for if I were doing that, certainly God would bless my evangelistic ministry.

My thoughts went back to seminary again. I recalled a professor of personal evangelism who used to keep our class spellbound by telling stories of how God had used him to win others to Christ. He would tell of how he would get on a bus, sit next to a total stranger and, by the time they got off the bus, the stranger would have accepted Christ. I was impressed!

So I got on a bus and took a seat next to a total stranger. By the time we got off the bus, he was mad at me! I was devastated.

For months and years during that first term of missionary service, I went through experience after experience like that. I wanted to be Bolivia's Billy Graham, but something was preventing me from doing it.

Then, little by little, I began to learn about spiritual gifts. A close missionary friend of mine, Kenneth Decker, of the New Testament Missionary Union, introduced me to Alex Hay's classic book, *The New Testament Order for Church and Missionary*. As I studied the book and the Scripture references it suggested, the biblical teaching on gifts began to come into focus. And then one day I made what I consider the most important spiritual discovery of my Christian life—*God had not given me the gift of evangelist!*

From that day on, I became a better Christian, a better missionary, a more joyous person, a better husband and father, and a more competent servant of God. To go back to Swindoll's fable, I was no longer an eagle trying to learn to climb a tree or a squirrel trying to learn how to fly. When I realized that in the Day of Judgment, God is not going to hold me accountable for what I did as an evangelist, I felt liberated. Guilt rolled off like the pack on the back of Christian in *Pilgrim's Progress*. It was God Himself who had not wanted me to be the Billy Graham of Bolivia. What a relief!

I had experimented with a spiritual gift. I had tried hard to use it. And I had come to the important discovery that I did not have the gift.

Let me hasten to say that, although I may not have the *gift* of evangelist, like every other Christian I do have a *role* of witness. Wherever I go and at all times I try to be a good representative of God. I know how to share Christ, and I occasionally lead a person to the Lord. Not having the gift of evangelist should never be a cop-out from consistent witnessing.

Using the Gifts Inventories

One of the best ways to determine which gifts to experiment with first is to take the Wagner-Modified Houts Questionnaire, which has been included in the back of this book and which is also available separately under the title *Finding Your Spiritual Gifts*. I designed this user-friendly tool years ago from a model first developed by Richard Houts. Now in its eighth revision, it is based on the definitions found in this book and it tests for 27 of the 28 gifts. The gift that I have been unsuccessful in testing for, after many attempts, is the gift of martyrdom. But the others usually are revealed fairly accurately.

Although a gifts inventory should never be considered the final word on discovering gifts, it does point in helpful directions. My questionnaire scores each gift from 0 to 15, and I suggest that people begin seriously experimenting with the 3 or 4 gifts that score highest.

STEP 3: EXAMINE YOUR FEELINGS

Somewhere along the line, personal feelings have fallen into disrepute with many believers. According to them, if someone is found enjoying life, something must be wrong. But things are changing. The new teaching on spiritual gifts is opening the way for an age in which serving God can be fun. I appreciate Ray Stedman for telling it like it is when he says, "Somewhere the idea has found deep entrenchment in Christian circles that doing what God wants you to do is always unpleasant; that Christians must always make choices between doing what they want to do and being happy and doing what God wants them to do and being completely miserable."[2] And Kenneth Kinghorn takes aim at the right target when he observes, "Maturing Christians grow beyond shallow concepts of discipleship that equate unhappiness with serving God."[3]

My concept is this: The same God who gives spiritual gifts also oversees the way each one of us is made up in our total being. God knows every detail of our psychological condition, our glands and hormones, our metabolism, our total personality. He understands our feelings perfectly. And He knows that if we enjoy doing a task, we do a better job at it than if we do not enjoy it. So part of God's plan, as I understand it, is to match the spiritual gifts He gives us with our temperament in such a way that if we really have those gifts, we will feel good using them. This may well be why, as we saw in chapter 2, God reserves the assigning of spiritual gifts to Himself. All the computers at IBM would not be equipped to assign gifts for the hundreds of millions of Christians around the world, but it is no problem to God Almighty.

Substantial biblical teaching also reveals that this is the way God wants to lead His people. Psalm 37:4 says, "Delight yourself also in the LORD, and He shall give you the desires of your heart." Philippians 2:13 adds, "For it is God who works in you both to will and to do for His good pleasure." Apparently, when people are doing God's will, they will be doing what they want to do. Biblically, then, it seems that we should not have a conflict between enjoying ourselves and pleasing God.

These concepts sparked Peyton Marshall to research and write a Ph.D. dissertation at St. Louis University entitled *The Measurement of Spiritual Gifts Using the Modified Houts Questionnaire.* In it he affirmed that the measurements proved accurate. He also referred to the doctoral research of Lawrence Selig of Luther-Northwestern Seminary, affirming that spiritual gifts "should have some correlation with the sixteen temperament types described by Isabel Myers."[4] This implies that God does, in fact, match our spiritual gifts to our temperament so that we will enjoy using them.

Findley Edge agrees. He says that a person who finds God's calling through his or her gift will get a eureka feeling. That means the person says, "This, really, is what I had rather do for God than anything else in the world."[5]

Edge points out that when we exercise a certain ministry, we subconsciously communicate the motivation behind the ministry to others. If the motivation is negative, those who receive the ministry may receive a negative message and the total effect is less than ideal. If a positive motivation comes across, the ministry is thereby enhanced and made more effective. This makes a great deal of sense.

During that same first term as a missionary, when I discovered I did not have the gift of evangelist, I also discovered, largely through feelings this time, that I did not have the gift of pastor.

My wife, Doris, and I were assigned by our mission to the small village of San José de Chiquitos, where, among other things, we were to plant a new church. We started the church, small and struggling as it was. But in the course of experimenting with pastoral work, I soon learned that I was not particularly well equipped to handle people's personal problems. When someone begins to tell me about his or her personal life, I become upset. I tend to worry about it, I lose sleep over it, I want to cry and I overreact in many ways. I make all the wrong moves. I cannot trust my intuitions. In a word, my feelings tell me God has not given me the gift.

Of course, I do have the role of occasionally helping others through their problems and relating in a pastoral way when certain situations occur. Members of my family, certain friends and, at times, students need my help, and I try to give it to them as best as I can. Realistically, however, my rate of success at personal counseling is extremely low, if not zero. And because I react so poorly, I tend to avoid counseling situations as much as possible. Some people find it hard to understand that listening to other people's problems can be a drain on emotional energies for those of us who do not have the gift of pastor.

After I realized that I do not have the gift of pastor, I did accept a pastorate. An important principle lay behind my acceptance, which Findley Edge expresses well when he says, "There are times when we must engage in action simply on the basis of 'ought.' A particular job needs to be done and a sense of 'ought' is the best (or only) motivation we have for doing it."[6] In my case, the "ought" was filling in as interim pastor of a large city church in Bolivia during the time that the pastor, Jaime Rios, was on leave of absence to coordinate the massive, nationwide Evangelism-in-Depth effort of 1965. Bolivia needed to be evangelized more strenuously, and because I believed so strongly in that goal, I was willing to do what needed to be done, although it meant ministering for a season on the basis of a role rather than a gift.

Although feelings may have to be put aside from time to time on the basis of an "ought" situation, it should only be temporary. The normal thing is for Christians to feel turned on by the work they are doing for God because they have discovered the spiritual gifts that God has given them. While experimenting with the gifts, then, it is important to examine your feelings.

STEP 4: EVALUATE YOUR EFFECTIVENESS

Spiritual gifts are task oriented, so it is not out of order to expect them to work. If God has given you a gift, He has done so because He wants you to accomplish something for Him in the context of the Body of Christ. Gifted people see results. Postulating that God wants us to be successful is not contradictory to sincere Christian humility. If you experiment with a gift and consistently find that what it is supposed to do does not happen, you probably have discovered another one of the gifts God has not given you.

This is where I got my first clue that I do not have the gift of evangelist. I tried to be an evangelist with dedication and sincerity, but it did not work. I tried public evangelism, and practically nobody was saved through my preaching. I tried personal evangelism, only to get knots in my stomach and to become tongue-tied. When I observed some of my friends who were

> ## When true gifts are in operation, whatever is supposed to happen through them *will* happen.

effortlessly witnessing and leading large numbers of people to Christ, I then knew that, compared to them, I was getting very little supernatural help in my attempts at evangelizing. I began to realize that I was attempting it in the flesh, not the Spirit. God was trying to tell me something.

If you have the gift of evangelist, people will come to Christ regularly through your ministry. If you have the gift of exhortation, you will help people through their problems and see lives straightened out. If you have the gift of healing, sick people will get well. If you have the gift of administration, the organization will run smoothly. When true gifts are in operation, whatever is supposed to happen through them *will* happen.

THE GIFT OF TEACHING

During our first term on the mission field, not only did I discover two gifts that I do not have, the gifts of evangelist and pastor; but I also discovered one gift that I do have, the gift of teaching.

I now have become conscious of the fact that when I get to the final judgment, God is going to ask me tough questions about what I did with the gift of teaching. Because I know the question is coming, I make it a point to do everything I can in this life to have a satisfactory answer ready.

> *The gift of teaching is the special ability that God gives to certain members of the Body of Christ to communicate information relevant to the health and ministry of the Body and its members in such a way that others will learn.*

You will see immediately that this definition has effectiveness built in—"others will learn." Always keep in mind the purpose of teaching. Michael Griffiths says, "Traditionally too much Christian teaching is pulpit soliloquy and nobody ever checks up to see whether anyone takes notice or whether teaching produces any action."[7] How true!

When I Teach, People Learn

Because I have the gift of teaching, I fully expect people to learn, both in my classes and through my writings. If I thought I would get any other kind of results, I would doubt that I had the gift. I hope I am not thinking more highly of myself than I ought to think. I honestly believe that I am thinking soberly when I say these things. I frequently get letters from students who write, "Your seminar was the best learning experience I have had since leaving seminary 20 years ago," or words to that effect. Frankly,

I expect that to happen, just as Billy Graham expects people to get up and go forward when he gives an evangelistic invitation. But I still love to get the letters.

That does not mean I never bomb. Unfortunately, I do. A while ago, for example, I was invited to conduct a seminar on church growth. I found out only after I arrived that many of those who had signed up were neither born-again Christians nor did they believe that fulfilling the Great Commission to make disciples of all nations was very important. By the end of the week, both the attendees and I were anxious to go home, and the evaluations that came in afterward were dismal. This is the exception, however. On a scale of 1 to 10, my ratings usually come out between 8 and 10, although in almost every class I rub some the wrong way, so they give me a 2 or a 3.

The gift of teaching is mentioned in all three of the primary lists of spiritual gifts: Romans 12, 1 Corinthians 12 and Ephesians 4. This does not mean that it is any more valid than a gift mentioned only once, but it probably does mean that it occurs more frequently in churches across the board. Although different churches may have different gift-mixes, I think virtually every church would have been given the gift of teacher as a part of its mix. I also think that the percentage of members of the Body of Christ who receive the gift of teacher might turn out to be higher than the percentage for many other gifts.

Varieties of Teaching

The gift of teaching comes in many varieties. For example, some people have a gift of teaching that enables them to communicate well to children. My gift is basically for adults, and, frankly, kids think I am a terrible bore. I make it a practice never to accept teaching invitations for young people of college age or below.

Others who have the gift of teaching are good at one-on-one teaching such as Paul with Timothy, or Aquila and Priscilla with Apollos (see Acts 18:26). I do a good bit of that as a mentor for theses and dissertations, but I have found that (1) I do not enjoy it much and (2) many others on our faculty do a far superior job than I. My strength is standing before a classroom of 30 or maybe 50 people. Beyond that, my effectiveness falls off. I do not believe I could ever match the kind of teaching Bill Gothard does, for example, who can hold the attention of 10,000 or 15,000 people through an intensive seminar.

Some people use their gift of teaching through media, such as the radio or television. Some are good at teaching laypeople; some are good at teaching professionals. Some teachers are able to use their gift through writing; others find writing a drag and do as little of it as possible. Some teach through the medium of preaching; others through drama.

Teaching is often a full-time gift. Unlike other gifts that may be used only occasionally, such as deliverance or discerning of spirits, and unlike celibacy, which is relatively passive once it is discovered and in operation, teaching usually implies a steady, regular use, requiring lots of time in study and preparation. Not only does that apply to professional teachers such as myself, but also to nonprofessional Sunday School teachers in the church. Sunday School teachers who have the gift of teaching will probably not be able to do very much more as far as ministry in the church is concerned, because those who have the gift of teaching love to spend large amounts of time studying the lesson. They work hard on details; they organize and reorganize. They search for illustrations that will make the material more meaningful. They spend time on visuals. For example, I find myself sometimes spending a considerable amount of time preparing a PowerPoint slide that I will use for only 15 or 30 seconds in a class. But if it nails down a point effectively, it is well worth it, and I feeel tremendous satisfaction.

Teachers who have the gift of teaching are patient with their students. They create an atmosphere in their classes that allows students to feel free to raise questions of any kind without feeling that they will be put down or made to look stupid before the others. True teachers have a fear of projecting any attitude that could be interpreted as manipulation or humiliation. They are not threatened or defensive when criticism comes. Such attitudes and intuitions are not the kind of thing that can be learned by just anyone. They are part of the supernatural dimension of having a spiritual gift.

STEP 5: EXPECT CONFIRMATION FROM THE BODY

If you think that you have a certain spiritual gift and you are trying to exercise it, but no one else in your church thinks you have it, you probably do not. It needs to be confirmed.

At this point, you might find a conflict between step 4, concerning your feelings, and step 5, concerning confirmation. Feelings are important, but they are far from infallible. You may have a deep desire to help other people, for example. You may feel strongly that God is calling you to minister through counseling or through the gift of exhortation. But if you are experimenting with counseling and you find over a period of time that few people seek you out for help or recommend their friends and relatives to you or write notes to you telling you how much you have helped them, you have good reason to doubt the validity of your feelings as far as this spiritual gift is concerned. Confirmation from the Body is a check on all the steps. It is number 5 in sequence, but in some ways it is the most important of all.

The gifts, according to our working definition, are given for use within the context of the Body. It is necessary, then, that other members of the Body have an important say in confirming your gift.

One of the reasons confirmation from the Body is so important is that it builds in a system of accountability for the use of gifts. Whereas it is true that we are ultimately accountable to God, more immediately we are accountable to each other, and we need to take this seriously. There is a depth of commitment here. Elizabeth O'Connor vividly describes this and points out that accountability is never comfortable: "Commitment at the point of my gifts means that I must give up being a straddler. . . . Life will not be the smorgasbord I have made it, sampling and tasting here and there."[8]

If you truly have the gift of administration or helps or evangelist or mercy or whatever, but nobody else knows it, you may get away with being lazy about using it and no one will know the difference. But once it is known and confirmed by the church, your friends will rightly expect to see it in action. This is why I pointed out earlier that a desire to work hard is a prerequisite for discovering spiritual gifts. When members of the Body confirm one another's gifts, more can be accomplished just on the basis of people working harder at what God has called them to do.

For some years, I thought I had the gift of administration. Somewhat against my will at first, I was talked into taking over the administration of the mission agency under which Doris and I were serving. As I experimented with administration, I began to enjoy it quite a bit. As far as feelings were concerned, it seemed like it might be a gift. Then, each time my position came up for confirmation at the annual field conference meeting, a good bit of disagreement occurred among fellow workers about my appointment; and when the vote came, I would barely squeak by. I needed someone who had the gift of exhortation to tell me to get out of administration and go back to teaching, but either that person was not there or I was not listening. So I continued for some years, and predictably the mission did not advance greatly under my management.

Only after I got back to the United States and read the book *The Making of a Christian Leader*, written by my friend Ted Engstrom, did I begin to understand clearly that I did not have the gift of administration. In this case, another member of the Body, Ted, confirmed to me that I did not have the gift, and I have been grateful to him ever since.

FIND YOUR SPIRITUAL GIFT!

This chapter has been so autobiographical that an explanation might be in order. As many evangelists have discovered, personal testimonies can be extremely helpful in motivating people, because the testimonies provide something of flesh and blood with which to identify. Abstract concepts are fine, but they rarely move people. My purpose in this chapter has been to help you see more clearly how you can begin the exciting process of discovering your spiritual gift or gift-mix.

As I said in the beginning, this approach to discovering spiritual gifts may not help everybody, but I am confident that it will help most. Let me illustrate how it can work by quoting a letter from one of the most successful church-growth pastors in the United Methodist Church, Joe Harding. At the time of this incident, Pastor Harding's church, the Central United Protestant Church of Richland, Washington, was one of the largest and fastest-growing churches of the Northwest, an area not particularly known for explosive church growth. Joe Harding had enrolled in a Doctor of Ministry church-growth seminar, which

I was teaching in the Eastern Washington Fuller extension center. The classes were meeting in Harding's own church facilities. A few days after the lecture on spiritual gifts and church growth, Harding wrote this letter:

> Your class was particularly helpful to me in making a major decision. Just a few days before the class I had received a telephone call from one of our denominational executives asking me to move to a national office in the Board of Discipleship in Nashville to head up a new program of evangelism. I was told that I was their first choice and they really wanted me to accept this responsibility. I am acquainted with the program and I am enthusiastic about it.
>
> However, as I weighed the matter very carefully it was clear to me that my gifts are not primarily in administration, but in preaching and teaching and in pastoring. When I measured my personal gifts against the requirements of this challenging job, it was very easy for me to decline and to feel that God was calling me to remain in this congregation to demonstrate the potential of dynamic and vital growth within the Methodist church.
>
> I was in agony when I first received the call, because I felt I could not decline such a challenging opportunity. Your emphasis on the joy that you find in exercising the gifts put the matter in an entirely different perspective. I find that tremendous joy in standing before the congregation that I preach to, Sunday after Sunday. I simply know that that is what God is calling me to do.
>
> So your class came at a most appropriate time in my life and I simply want to share my gratitude with you.[9]

The thrill I got from receiving Joe Harding's letter could not have been any less than that which Billy Graham must feel when 3,000 people come forward in one of his crusades. I now thank God that I am not the Billy Graham of Bolivia, as I once thought I might be. God had something much better for *me*. He has a similar exciting and fulfilling thing in mind for *you*.

REFLECTIONS

1. What is your church's written or unwritten policy regarding spiritual gifts? Why is it important to belong to a church that has a position on spiritual gifts with which you agree?
2. Experimenting with spiritual gifts is an important step toward discovering whether you have them. Name two or three gifts you feel you might experiment with in the near future.
3. After you do the above, also name two or three gifts you have negative personal feelings about, strong enough so that you would not care even to experiment with them. How legitimate are these feelings?
4. Name those in your church who in all probability have the gift of teaching. What do they do that makes you point them out?
5. This chapter is about gift discovery. Can you, at this point, name a gift that you think God has given you? Which one? Why do you say that?

Notes
1. Ray C. Stedman, *Body Life* (Ventura, CA: Regal Books, 1972), p. 54.
2. Ibid.

3. Kenneth Cain Kinghorn, *Gifts of the Spirit* (Nashville, TN: Abingdon Press, 1976), p. 110.
4. Peyton R. Marshall, *The Measurement of Spiritual Gifts Using the Modified Houts Questionnaire* (Ann Arbor, MI: University Microfilms, 1987), p. 31.
5. Findley B. Edge, *The Greening of the Church* (Dallas: Word Books, 1971), p. 141.
6. Ibid., p. 142.
7. Michael Griffiths, *Cinderella's Betrothal Gifts* (Robesonia, PA: OMF Books, 1978), p. 36.
8. Elizabeth O'Connor, *Eighth Day of Creation* (Dallas: Word Books, 1971), pp. 42-43.
9. Joseph Harding, letter to the author, n.d.

Chapter 6

THE PASTOR'S GIFT-MIX

Up to this point, our treatment of spiritual gifts has been somewhat general. Important groundwork needed to be laid. It is impossible to be specific about spiritual gifts and how they function in the church unless the fog of ignorance about spiritual gifts is first dispelled. From time to time, I have mentioned certain ways that spiritual gifts relate to the church growth, but the stress has been on the general health of the individual Christians and their churches. Of course, the Church as a whole must be healthy if it is to grow well, but in many cases churches are not growing, largely because they experience an unhealthy problem concerning the operation of spiritual gifts.

For the expansion of the Church, locally and worldwide, four gifts above others are primary: the gift of pastor, the gift of evangelist, the gift of missionary and the gift of apostle.

THE KEY TO GROWTH

Let's begin with the pastor. As far as the growth of the local church is concerned (the spread of the gospel on new ground will be discussed in chapter 8), the pastor is the key person.

In the first book I wrote on American church growth, *Your*

Church Can Grow, I described seven vital signs of a healthy church, and I named the pastor as the first vital sign. When I wrote this back in 1976, I wondered how the hypothesis would hold up under the scrutiny of other professionals in the field. Feedback over the decades has caused me to modify some of my postulations on other vital signs, but if anything, the hypothesis about the pastor being the key person for growth of the local church has been strengthened. Few experts disagree.

Since that book was written, significant studies have been published on the growth trends of three of our major mainline denominations: the United Methodist Church, the Presbyterian Church (USA) and the Southern Baptist Convention. They all have verified the crucial role of the pastor.

The Methodist study, for example, speaks of the several organizations that specialized in studying church growth: "In one way or another, they all recognize the pastor is the key person. They may disagree about how the pastor should be involved, but they all agree that the pastor should be involved." Many reasons can be given for this, but the study highlights one of them by arguing that "the pastor's involvement signals his or her commitment to the conviction that one of the most important tasks of the local congregation is that of extending the ministry of the church to include more persons."[1]

The Presbyterian study, after analyzing causes of decline and growth, sets forth 10 "implications for positive action" that the authors believe the Presbyterian Church must take if it is to reverse the general downward trend of church membership. The first deals with motivation (the church must affirm that it expects growth), but the second deals with the pastor. It argues, "The United Presbyterian Church must adequately recognize strong pastoral competence as a decisive factor for the vitality and outreach of a congregation." The study mentions that all their formal and informal research leads to the same conclusion, namely "pastoral leadership is crucial to almost all aspects of vital congregational life, and certainly to membership growth."[2] When they compare the perceptions of members of growing churches to members of declining churches, they find that pastors of growing churches are seen to be taking more responsibility for church growth, having more influence on what happens in the church, promoting a sense of unity and more able to handle conflict.

The most comprehensive test of the seven vital signs was conducted by the Home Mission Board of the Southern Baptist Convention in 1977. The convention designed and carried out a computerized study of 30,029 Southern Baptist churches to find out which were the 425 fastest growing in the denomination. A special study was made of these, seeing if Wagner's vital signs fit. In-depth case studies were then carried on in the 15 churches that showed the best growth records to compare them to the general data. Concerning the first vital sign, the role of the pastor, the report states, "Pastors of the top 15 fastest growing churches agree the key is leadership. . . . While giving credit to others, all say they are responsible to God for the growth, nurture, direction, outreach and ministry of the church. They feel they are God's man in God's church in God's time."[3]

Between 1976 and 1978, the Hartford Seminary Foundation gathered a top-level research team of sociologists of religion, church planners and denominational executives to study why mainline denominations in the United States had been declining since 1965. One of their conclusions was "Both wisdom and the available hard data clearly converge to tell us that the role of pastor is critical for 'growing' a congregation."[4]

Understandably, some pastors react negatively to the hypothesis that they are the key person for growth in their churches. Although some resistance to this may emerge from true humility, probably much more needs to be attributed to reluctance on the part of many pastors to shoulder so much responsibility. They would rather pass the buck, so to speak. In neither case, however, are the objections adequate. Church people in general are beginning to realize more than ever before that those who accept the responsibility of being the pastor of a church also accept the primary responsibility for its growth or decline, just as much as an airplane pilot accepts responsibility for keeping the plane in the air during flight. The airplane won't fly without wings and stabilizer and engine, true. But recognizing that does not change the fact that the pilot is the one who makes it fly.

Theologically, it is true that Jesus is the head of the Church. But He also chooses and equips His undershepherds. A church structure may have 100 or 500 or 5,000 members, but one person above all others in that church is most directly answerable to Jesus Christ, the head of the universal Church, for the welfare of the particular local church body. That person, of course, is the pastor.

This is why pastoral gift-mixes are so crucial for church growth. Given the right person with the right gift-mix, virtually any church has possibilities for growth.

THE MYTH OF THE OMNICOMPETENT PASTOR

An outmoded view of the pastor's role, although diminishing, strongly persists in some circles today. It is the view that the pastor is hired by the congregation to do all the ministry of the church. The better the pastor, the more the people of the church can relax and become spectators. It is not only an outmoded view, but it is also unbiblical.

The Bible's view of the Body of Christ is that it is an organism in which all the members function together. The best pastor is not one who relieves members of their ministries, but one who makes sure that each member has a ministry and is working hard at it.

The pastor is only one of many members of the Body. Only Jesus is the head, but the pastor may be something like the nervous system that carries messages from the head to the various members of the body and makes sure they are all working together in harmony. The smooth coordination of the Body uniquely depends on the pastor. Many church members do not recognize or accept this. Although they may not expect their pastors to do everything, they expect them to do most things. Many church people believe the stereotype that pastors need to be accomplished public speakers, skilled counselors, biblical and theological scholars, public relations experts, administrators, social ethicists, masters of ceremony, soul winners, funeral directors and stimulating teachers, and to be competent at everything else except perhaps walking on water. Hundreds of pulpit committees are misguidedly searching for this "omnicompetent" pastor.

Of course, they never find such a pastor. Anyone at all conversant with spiritual gifts could predict this. No one in the Body has all the gifts, pastors included. When this simple fact is overlooked, though, disappointment is right around the corner. Such disappointment is not really necessary. It can be avoided if and when pastoral responsibility is evaluated and job descriptions for church ministries are written on the basis of spiritual gifts.

QUALITIES OF A CHURCH GROWTH PASTOR

The report from the Hartford Seminary Foundation includes another statement significant to our discussion: "Unfortunately they are less clear in telling us specifically what it is about that role or about the qualities of the person filling that role that is most important." One of the precise purposes of this chapter is to identify the qualities of a church growth pastor that the study did not uncover. I certainly do not have all the answers, but I think that by explaining them in the context of spiritual gifts, I can at least make a reasonable start in describing some of the qualities a church growth pastor should have.

What, then, are the spiritual gifts necessary for a successful, church growth pastor? It might be best to approach this question first of all from the negative viewpoint. What gifts are *not* necessary for the pastor of a growing church? My suggestion is that only 2 of the 28 gifts are indispensable for the pastor of a rapidly growing church. This leaves 26 gifts that are, shall we say, optional. It is not necessary to list all 26 gifts that a successful pastor may or may not have. Four of them, however, do deserve mention because they are four qualities that many people mistakenly think a church growth pastor needs: the gifts of pastor, exhortation, evangelist and administration.

THE GIFT OF PASTOR

Until now, I have been using the word "pastor" in its broad, contemporary sense. In current vocabulary, it signifies the person who is the designated head of a local church. He or she is alternately called the minister, the rector, the parson, the vicar, the reverend or sometimes the preacher. From now on, as far as this gift is concerned, we need to use "pastor" in a more technical sense.

Some people think it is odd when they first hear that a successful pastor does not need the pastoral gift. In fact, very few senior ministers of large, growing churches do have the biblical gift of pastor. Almost by definition, if pastors of large churches had the gift, they would not be where they are. And those who do head up large churches and still have a pastoral gift frequently find it a source of frustration. If not properly handled and understood, the gift of pastor often becomes a cause of nongrowth, as we will see shortly.

But, first, what is the pastoral gift?

The gift of pastor is the special ability that God gives to certain members of the Body of Christ to assume a long-term personal responsibility for the spiritual welfare of a group of believers.

The Meaning of "Pastor"

The word "pastor" itself is borrowed from animal husbandry, particularly sheep raising. It is by no means as universally an understood vocation today as it was in first-century Palestine, so it may need some explanation. A pastor is the person responsible under Jesus—who is the master shepherd—for teaching a group of Christians, feeding them, healing their wounds, developing unity, helping them find their gifts and doing whatever else is necessary to see that they continue in the faith and grow in their spiritual lives.

Several biblical words are used as synonyms for "pastor." The English words "elder," "presbyter," "overseer" and "bishop" (sometimes interchanged depending on the translation) have the same meaning as "pastor." Because these words are used in such a variety of ways in our contemporary churches, it is helpful to distinguish between the *office* of pastor and the *gift* of pastor. Most of those whom we call pastors in America are people occupying the *office* of pastor. They have a staff position in the church. The point I am making here is that not everyone who has the *office* of pastor, as understood today, needs the *gift* of pastor. Furthermore, many men and women who have the *gift* of pastor have not been given the *office* of pastor by having been placed on a church staff.

Pastoring, Preaching and Teaching

Note that "preaching" has not been listed as a spiritual gift. Perhaps it could be, but I do not feel it would be any more useful than adding "making movies" or "radio broadcasting" or "writing." All of these are forms of communications media that can be used for the exercise of any number of the more substantial gifts. Through preaching, for example, some exercise their gift of evangelist, some their gift of teaching, some their gift of faith, others their gift of healing and so forth. We often require competent preaching as a quality for those we hire to occupy the office of pastor, and nothing is wrong with that. But many people, if not most, who have the gift of pastor will not be accomplished preachers. Although preachers tend to draw the attention of others to themselves, pastors tend to pour out their attention on others.

And another thing: The gift of pastor is frequently attached to teacher in the hyphenated pastor-teacher gift-mix, as we saw in Ephesians 4:11, but the two gifts can and do operate independently of each other as well. Teaching can involve a short-term relationship between student and teacher, maybe in a one-day seminar, and still be done well. Pastoring implies a much more patient and personal relationship over the long haul. Churches do not hire a person to come in for a week to do pastoral work in the same way that they may hire an evangelist or a Bible teacher. A teacher can have a low need for people, but a pastor typically has a high need for people. A teacher can be content oriented, motivation oriented or task oriented. A pastor usually is person oriented.

As soon as we understand that the gift of pastor is not necessarily what your senior minister has or needs, a vast and exciting possibility is opened for laypeople to begin to exercise the gift of pastor. In many churches, the gift of pastor has not been recognized among laypeople simply because no one has looked for it. The assumption has been that when churches hire pastors and pay them salaries, they are paying them to do the "pastoral" work. By doing so, they may be undercutting the growth of their church and not understand why.

A Universal, Gender-Based Gift

I believe that the gift of pastor is a universal gift. In other words, probably every local church of any substance has the gift of pastor included in its gift-mix. This may not be true of some parachurch organizations, but it is necessarily true of churches. Ample New Testament teachings show how pastors or elders were provided by God for every church. Paul saw that they were identified and properly ordained even in the very young churches he started as a foreign missionary. Acts 14:23, for example, tells us that Paul and his fellow missionaries ordained elders (pastors) in "every church."

I further believe that the gift of pastor is given to both men and women. My lifetime observation of churches in many cultures leads me to believe that this is usually another of the gender-biased gifts. More women, I think, have the gift of pastor than men. Take, as a starter, David Yonggi Cho's Yoido Full Gospel Church in Seoul, Korea, which for years was the largest local church in the world. Women do more than 80 percent of the pastoral work in that church.

CHURCH GROWTH AND
THE GIFT OF PASTOR

Now we are ready for the question How many people in the Body—women and men—should we expect have been given the gift of pastor? And then, How does this gift relate directly to the growth or nongrowth of churches?

Celebration-Congregation-Cell

It is helpful to think of the gift of pastor as essentially a congregational gift. Here I am using the word "congregation" in terms of the celebration-congregation-cell structure, which I described in *Your Church Can Grow* as one of the seven vital signs of a healthy church.[5] The "celebration," usually the Sunday morning worship service, which brings together all those who belong to the membership circle of the church, is not limited in size except by secondary considerations. The "congregation," which brings together people in fellowship circles, has an optimum size of between 35 and 80 members. The "cell," where personal intimacy and accountability take place on a deeper level, should run between 8 and 12 people. Cells take various forms. For example, in most Southern Baptist churches, Sunday School classes often function as cells. In many other churches, they meet in homes.

Although the person who has the *office* of pastor, or the senior minister, usually leads the celebration, a pastoral gift is not required for that particular function. On the other side of the spectrum, the home cell group, when operating properly, draws each of the members into a mutual caring dynamic, which requires only the *role* of pastor on the part of each of the members, not necessarily a person with the *gift*. The spiritual gift of pastor is not essential, then, to the well-being of either the celebration or the cell.

Pastoring the "Congregation"

In that intermediate structure, the congregation, however, is where the pastoral gift can become most relevant and find its fullest expression. Churches that range from 100 to 250 members and seem to be having growth problems would do well to take a close look at this particular area of their church life. One of their problems might be that they have only one congregation, when they need several, and that the requirements for pastoral care have already been stretched past the available resources.

What do I mean specifically?

A part-time layperson who has the gift of pastor can usually handle from 8 to 15 families in his or her flock, so to speak. The exact number depends on the degree of the gift they have, on the time available each week to use that gift and on the cell or small group dynamic operating in the church. A professionally trained, full-time minister who also has the gift of pastor can usually handle between 50 and 100 families, depending again on the degree of the gift and on the other responsibilities included in the job description.

Suppose that in a large church there is a "congregation" of 100 members consisting of 40 couples and 20 single adults. It may be an adult Bible class, a Sunday School department, a choir or a geographical grouping—all these and others are common structures for congregations. If it is a larger church, chances are that the members of this congregation will not have day-to-day access to the senior minister or to other staff members in a pastoral relationship. If I belong to a church of 4,500 members, for example, I may have lunch with the senior minister about once a year and consider myself highly privileged, because lunch is served only 365 days in a year. In no way should the minister be expected to pastor 4,500 people or to get to know them all personally.

How Many Have the Pastoral Gift?

In a large church, pastoral care on a congregational level—a scale much smaller than the entire membership circle—becomes crucial. In our hypothetical congregation of 100 members, then, it would be reasonable to expect that God would have given the gift of pastor to possibly 4 or 5 members of that particular segment of the Body of Christ. They would ordinarily be laypersons who would become directly responsible for the spiritual welfare of families in the congregation. They would be selected for this on the basis of the spiritual gifts God has given them, particularly the gift of pastor. They should also have some sort of formal, public recognition of that gift. If ordination is out of order, then some sort of commissioning or public consecration will suffice. The designation as a member of the pastoral care team is usually adequate. But the point is that these gifts must be confirmed by the Body and set into action. God has already done His part by giving the gifts.

Now let's move from the larger church where the gift of pastor needs to be operative in a number of subcongregations to smaller churches where the membership group may be identical to the fellowship group. In other words, a one-congregation church. How is the growth of such a church affected by the gift of pastor?

Church A and Church B

Consider Church A. It has 200 members and has been at that level for some years. The pastor of the church also happens to have the gift of pastor.

Now consider Church B. Likewise it has 200 members and has plateaued. But in this case, either the pastor does not have the gift of pastor, or is serving part-time (as are, for example,

10,000 bivocational Southern Baptist pastors in America) and cannot exercise the gift very much even if it were present.

In Church A, because the pastor has the gift and loves to use it, he or she is likely to give a great deal of time to the members in visitation and meeting with groups and social activities. In such churches, pastors are usually more people oriented than task oriented. They may emphasize "relational theology" in their messages. They may spend only a minimal time, if any, in working out growth goals for the church and in planning how the goals can be implemented. They may not want to do this planning because they realize they are at best doing a substandard job of pastoring their 200 members. As we have said, even a full-time professional can handle only 50 to 100 families, and Church A has reached the upper limit.

If pastors of churches such as Church A think they do not need any help in pastoring the flock, the chances are the church will not grow. Regardless of how much they may make public pronouncements about reaching the unchurched and winning souls, being relevant to the community and adding to the church membership, they unconsciously may make sure such does not happen. This has no malicious intent whatsoever. It grows out of a sincere desire to serve the Lord by using the gifts they have. Such pastors would likely imagine that they could do a higher quality job of pastoring if the flock had *fewer* members, not *more*.

God calls many, many pastors to shepherd a flock like Church A. In fact, 80 to 90 percent of churches in America and around the world fit this description. Pastor, if God has called you and equipped you to be a small church pastor, obey Him, be a good pastor; and your Master will say, "Well done, good and faithful servant."

How about Church B? If those who are hired as pastors of churches are either part-time or do not have the gift of pastor and they try to do the pastoral work themselves, the church will most likely decline over a period of two or three years. Ministers without the gift of pastor can be expected to make every effort to arrange their schedule so that they keep busy in other good spiritual activities, which leaves them little time for pastoral work. They may prefer to prepare expository sermons than to visit the hospital. They may give a great deal of attention to administrative details and not be available much for counseling. They may feel more comfortable carrying their Christian witness to the community through civic organizations than spending much time with the fellowship groups in the church or in homes. If this is the case, and the pastoral work thereby suffers, the health of the Body is damaged, and decline may be just around the corner.

> # Pastor without the gift of pastor, the Lord Himself has given your church all the pastoral gifts it needs.

But in the final analysis, Church B actually has a higher potential for growth than Church A. If it occurs to Church B that God may have provided spiritual gifts to laypeople in the congregation to do the work that the pastor dislikes, the pastor would be elated. If, on the other hand, someone suggested this same thing to pastors of churches like Church A, the pastors might feel threatened. Because of their spiritual gift, these pastors love personal pastoral work so much that they do not care to be freed to do something else. For pastors of churches like Church B, just the opposite is likely. They would feel liberated. They could do what they like to do and still keep their job.

Take heart, Pastor without the gift of pastor! The Lord Himself has given your church all the pastoral gifts it needs. God is depending on you to see that the gifts are actuated. You have accepted the leadership of the church. In your church of 200 members, you can assume that God has given the gift of pastor to around six or eight women and men whose Christian lives will be more abundantly fulfilled than ever when they are properly equipped and encouraged. They are waiting to be put to work in ministry. They will do a better job of caring for the sheep than you can, seminary degree and all. Get them involved and ministering. Provide any training they need. They will be happier and more productive—and they will love you for it.

THE GIFT OF EXHORTATION

The gift of exhortation, like the gift of pastor, is a person-centered gift. An individual can manifest it in two ways: (1) in a preaching/teaching context or in a group encounter; or (2) in a private one-on-one situation that meets the particular need of a particular person at a particular time.

The gift of exhortation, however, is different from the gift of pastor in that a flock or a group of people is not necessarily involved on the basis of a long-term commitment. A person who has the gift of exhortation becomes concerned with the spiritual welfare of a brother or sister for the period of time it takes to help that person; then he or she moves on to another. The gift of exhortation can operate with relative strangers, but the pastoral gift cannot. Exhortation and pastoral gifts may, of course, both be part of the same person's gift-mix, and perhaps this is a frequent occurrence.

The gift of exhortation—sometimes called the gift of counseling— is the special ability that God gives to certain members of the Body of Christ to minister words of comfort, consolation, encouragement and counsel to other members of the Body in such a way that they feel helped and healed.

A prominent biblical example of someone who had the gift of exhortation was Paul's associate Barnabas, who was called "Son of Encouragement" (Acts 4:36). Barnabas was the one who took Paul under his wing when the other apostles were skeptical about the validity of Paul's conversion. Barnabas saw the potential in John Mark and picked him up after Paul had rejected him. As Leslie Flynn points out, "Do we realize that had not Barnabas used his gift of encouragement we might be missing half of the New Testament books?"[6] Barnabas never wrote Scripture, but two people he helped did. Paul contributed 13 epistles, and Mark contributed one Gospel.

CHURCH GROWTH AND THE GIFT OF EXHORTATION

All Christians, of course, have a role of caring for one another. Hebrews 3:13 says, "Exhort one another daily." The lifestyle of Christians should be to counsel, share and encourage one another at all times. But over and above this *role*, some have a special *gift* of counseling (exhortation) that should become recognized to the extent that people in the church who are hurting know where to go to find help. When this happens, the Body is in good health.

Church pastors do not necessarily need the gift of exhortation to lead a church into vigorous growth. This gift, like the spiritual gift of pastor, could be a hindrance to growth if the senior minister has it. For example, the United Methodist report on membership trends suggests that one of its growth problems might be the "large number of pastors now serving in the United Methodist Church who have been strongly influenced by an emphasis on their role as a passive counselor. Ministers who operate from this stance are not inclined to confront persons with the claims of the gospel or to press for a decision to unite with the church."[7]

Because of the emphasis made on nondirective counseling and relational theology in many seminaries, some pastors who do not have either the *gift* of pastor or the *gift* of exhortation may be overstressing their need to exercise a *role* in these areas. When the implications of suggestions such as those made in the Methodist report are understood, churches may recognize that they must retool and readjust their ministerial priorities at this point, if they are to grow over future decades.

If this happens, we will begin to recognize that the gift of exhortation is another of those gifts that many laypersons in the church have. The gift should be identified and put to use, and the pastor is the one most responsible to see that this is done. Sometimes it might be advisable to hire a professional counselor for the church staff if the church is big enough to afford it. But this is not always necessary. The resources for meeting the needs for counseling may already be right there in the congregation in the form of the gift of exhortation, waiting to be uncovered and used.

THE GIFT OF ADMINISTRATION

Two other gifts frequently, but mistakenly, considered necessary for the pastor of a growing church are the gifts of evangelist and administration. I will postpone discussing the gift of evangelist for the next chapter, but here I would like to touch on the gift of administration.

I like to use the term "the gift of administration" instead of "the gift of governments," as the *King James Version* has it in the list of gifts in 1 Corinthians 12:28, because "administration" better describes my own interpretation of the gift and its place in a healthy church. A different Greek word is used in the list in Romans 12, translated as "ruling" in the *King James Version* (v. 8), which, based upon the *New King James Version*, I am calling the gift of leadership. In other words, I am distinguishing between the gift of *administration* and the gift of *leadership*. I believe that a church growth pastor can get along without the gift of administration but not very well without the gift of leadership.

The gift of administration is the special ability that God gives to certain members of the Body of Christ to understand clearly the immediate and long-range goals of a particular unit of the Body and to devise and execute effective plans for the accomplishment of those goals.

The Greek word for "administration" is the nautical word for the ship's captain. The captain is the person in charge of getting the ship to its destination. That is a perfect description of the person to whom God has given the gift of administration. The captain stands between the owner of the ship and the crew. The owner of the ship makes the basic decisions about the purpose of the voyage, what the ship will carry, where the ship is going and what it will do when it gets there. The owner sees that a captain is hired and monitors the competency of the captain. The crew, on the other hand, takes orders from the captain and does the physical work necessary for the captain to get the ship to its destination. When trouble occurs in midvoyage, the owner is not consulted, unless it is a dire emergency. The captain is expected to make the decisions necessary to solve problems as they arise so that the goals are accomplished and the ship gets to where the owner wants it.

In this analogy, it is clear to me that pastors of growing churches are equivalent to the owners of ships. They need to know where the ship should go and why. They need to locate a captain and recruit a crew. But they do not necessarily have to be or want to be a captain, to say nothing about a member of the crew, for the total purpose to be accomplished.

Pastors who have the gift of administration can make a church organization hum. They enjoy spending long hours in the office, overseeing the business matters of the church, relating to staff, making phone calls, closing deals, sending and receiving e-mails and taking satisfaction in their organization. But pastors who do not enjoy any of the above need not despair. In small churches, God may have given gifts of administration to men and women who would love to exercise them as a contribution to the church. Sometimes God provides a church secretary who has the gift. In larger churches, a skilled assistant is often added to the staff.

THE GIFT OF FAITH

If successful pastors of large, growing churches *do not need* 26 of the spiritual gifts, the remaining two they *do need* must be significant. I believe they are. They are the gift of faith and the gift of leadership.

> *The gift of faith is the special ability that God gives to certain members of the Body of Christ to discern with extraordinary confidence the will and purposes of God for the future of His work.*

People who have the gift of faith are usually more interested in the future than in history. They are goal-oriented, possibility thinkers, undaunted by circumstances, suffering or obstacles. They can trust God to remove mountains as 1 Corinthians 13:2 indicates. They, like Noah, can obey God by building an ark on dry ground in the face of ridicule and criticism, having no doubt at all that God is going to send a flood.

People who have the gift of faith are often highly irritated by criticism, much more, for example, than those who have the gift of teaching. They cannot bring themselves to understand why anyone would criticize them, because they have such complete assurance that what they are doing is God's will. They tend to interpret criticism of themselves as criticism of God, and therefore they often become impatient with friends who do not go along with them. They typically have difficulty understanding the "system" and why it seems to work as it does to slow down progress. Usually, people who have the gift of faith have a large amount of courage, because they feel deeply that they are in partnership with God, for "if God is for us, who can be against us?" (Rom. 8:31).

MEGACHURCH PASTORS

The megachurch pastors I know all have the gift of faith. Sometimes they are called visionaries, dreamers or promoters. They see where God wants them to go, although they may have no idea at that moment how they are going to get there. Years ago, I was aghast when I first heard Robert Schuller tell of his vision of a "crystal cathedral" in Garden Grove, California. A building of 10,000 pieces of glass, shaped like a diamond, larger than the Notre Dame Cathedral of Paris, having fountains of water down the center aisle—this blew my mind. But before I heard about his vision, I had already come to the conclusion that God had given Robert Schuller the gift of faith. If I had not been convinced of his gift, I would have thought that his mental health was questionable. But I took him seriously right from the beginning; in fact, Doris and I were among the first to buy one of the 10,000 pieces of glass when they were offered "for sale" to the public a number of years ago.

Robert Schuller reminds me of the late George Müller of Bristol, England, whom I mentioned in chapter 4. They both are examples of the gift of faith's being demonstrated in their ministries. Müller, in the nineteenth century, clearly saw God's will for orphanages and was undaunted by multiple obstacles, including a 5-million-dollar price tag. The money all came in during his lifetime. Schuller, in the twentieth century, clearly saw God's will for a beautiful sanctuary and likewise was undaunted by a multimillion-dollar price tag.

Schuller and Müller are similar in some ways but different in others. Müller adopted a policy of never making direct appeals for funds, but his ministry became known and funds poured in. He was fortunate enough to have the gift of intercession to accompany his gift of faith. Schuller takes the opposite approach. He tells of how he engaged a rich man in conversation, challenged him with the vision of the crystal cathedral, looked him in the eye and said, "I need your help. I would like you to give me a million dollars toward the cathedral." The man looked back at him and said, "Schuller, if you're crazy enough to ask me for a million dollars, I'm crazy enough to give it to you!" Within a few weeks, the million-dollar gift was in the bank. George Müller would likely have turned over in his grave. But God, I believe, is pleased with both of these heroes of faith.

PROJECTING THE GIFT OF FAITH

People who have the gift of faith may have a particular temptation of which both they and others around them need to be aware. They may easily fall into the syndrome of gift projection. Kenneth Kinghorn of Asbury Seminary warns, "The person who has the gift of faith should not chide others for their lack of faith. After all, not every Christian possesses this gift."[8]

I have already mentioned how guilty I would feel after reading a biography of George Müller until I understood something about gifts. Sometimes when I listen to Robert Schuller, I get a similar message. It sounds like: "If you do what I do, you will accomplish what I accomplish. It's easy." Now through many years of association, I have learned a great deal about possibility thinking from Schuller, and it has proven to be valuable in many aspects of my life. But it is far beyond me to spend time attempting to dream the kind of dreams that seem so natural and easy for him. King David refused to wear Saul's armor, and so do I. I do not regard myself as an impossibility thinker. I try to be a possibility thinker within the limits of my daily Christian role of faith without feeling any particular remorse that God may not do the kind of things through me that He is doing through my good friend. The whole body cannot be an eye.

Whenever we discuss the gift of faith, we often bring up names of the notables, such as Schuller and Müller. If more space were available, we could write a modern-day Hebrews 11, mentioning Ralph Winter, Bill Bright, Oral Roberts, Cameron Townsend, T. D. Jakes and David Yonggi Cho, who have all given public demonstration of their gift of faith, often measured by multimillion-dollar projects. This could and does easily become discouraging to other members of the Body of Christ who have a lesser degree of the gift of faith. But in God's family there are many more 1- or 2-talent people than there are 5- or 10-talent people.

Average people who have the gift of faith in a leadership role in the church may never build a crystal cathedral, but they can discern with a remarkable confidence where God wants the church to be 5 or 10 years later. They can set bold goals. They can establish a mood for growth. Because pastors such as these believe so strongly in growth, the people in their congregations find their attitude contagious. They get excited about it. The two basic axioms of church growth are (1) the pastor must want the church to grow and be willing to pay the price; and (2) the people must want the church to grow and be willing to pay the price. In a church where the pastor has the gift of faith, these two axioms are usually in dynamic operation. The church is ready to grow.

THE GIFT OF **LEADERSHIP**

The gift of faith helps church growth pastors know where they should go. The gift of leadership helps them know how to get there.

> *The gift of leadership is the special ability that God gives to certain members of the Body of Christ to set goals in accordance with God's purpose for the future and to communicate these goals to others in such a way that they voluntarily and harmoniously work together to accomplish those goals for the glory of God.*

Leaders must have followers. If leadership quality is due to a gift (in contrast to some legal power or position), the leaders' followers will be voluntary. Whereas discerning leaders never get too far ahead of their followers, they are always up front directing others. Gifted leaders neither manipulate nor coerce. They generate a confidence that they know where they are going and what the next step is to get there. Most people want to be led, and they willingly allow their leaders to influence them.

The best leaders are relaxed. They know what has to be done, and they know they cannot do it themselves, so they develop skills in delegating and transferring responsibilities to others. Many leaders dislike administration, so they make sure that they have delegated that responsibility to people who have administration in their gift-mix. Lyle Schaller likens skillful pastors of growing churches to ranchers, rather than shepherds. Ranchers make sure that their different flocks and herds get the attention they need, and they recruit others to do it. They take minimal personal interest in the problems of the individual sheep. Pastors who prefer the shepherd model will have to content themselves with churches that have a membership of under 200 people, and this may well be God's will for them. In them, their *role* of leadership will suffice without a special *gift*. On the other hand, those who can fit into the rancher model have much greater possibilities for growth. They are likely to have the gift of leadership. God loves both shepherds and ranchers.

It takes time to establish leadership in a church, even when the pastor has the gift of leadership. This is the main reason why pastoral longevity has been found to be directly related to church growth. A common thread running through the testimonies of pastors of churches that have established a reputation of excellence and growth is that they have more frequently than not received a lifetime call to that church. Neither the pastors nor their people wonder where the pastors will be five years later. Their commitment to each other is reminiscent of a marriage agreement—until death do us part. Lyle Schaller puts it this way: "One of the means of reducing the positive impact of pastoral leadership is to change ministers every few years."[9] He goes on to say that the most productive years of a pastor usually begin only between the third to sixth year of the minister's tenure.

Changing pastors frequently prevents a church from establishing a firm philosophy of ministry, which now is recognized as an important factor for the church's health and growth. Each church needs to be able to articulate why it is there and why it is not the same as other churches in a given area of ministry or in the same denomination. Few churches, however, have been able to establish their philosophy of ministry because competent pastoral leadership is needed in order to do it well. When pastors come and go frequently, philosophies of ministry usually come and go as well, and none of them amounts to very much.

When a church has a long-term pastoral commitment, the philosophy of ministry can and should be built around the spiritual gifts of the senior minister. Growing churches are doing this. A number of years ago, for example, I surveyed the Los Angeles area. I saw that Pastors John MacArthur and Charles Swindoll each had the gift of teaching. Their churches, Grace Community Church and First Evangelical Free Church, had a philosophy of ministry called classroom churches. Pastor John Wimber, on the other hand, built his Vineyard Christian Fellowship on a new, contemporary worship style geared to baby boomers that was combined with ministries of signs and wonders. All of these pastors, incidentally, had the gift of leadership.

THE VALUE OF A
SPIRITUAL-GIFTS DYNAMIC

Those who accept positions as pastors of Christian churches commit themselves to a life of demanding work. Not only must pastors discover and develop and use their own spiritual gifts, but also, even in the best of situations, they must be prepared to exercise Christian roles to a degree far above what is expected of the average Christian. This cannot be avoided.

If pastors do not develop a spiritual-gifts dynamic among

the members of the congregation, the pastors' use of the roles can easily become excessive. Ray Stedman laments that pastors have been assigned the task of "evangelizing the world, counseling the distressed and brokenhearted, ministering to the poor and needy, relieving the oppressed and afflicted, expounding the Scriptures, and challenging the entrenched forces of evil in an increasingly darkened world." He points out that pastors were never meant to do all this and that "to even attempt it is to end up frustrated, exhausted, and emotionally drained."[10] Is he describing your pastor?

Few things make the pastoral task more enjoyable than a congregation in which spiritual gifts are in operation. The pastor becomes the coach of the team. They are doing what they like to do and are doing it well. Growth possibilities are almost unlimited. The Body is functioning as its Maker designed it to function.

REFLECTIONS

1. Although research confirms that the pastor is the principal key to the growth of the local church, some pastors, nevertheless, deny that it is true. Why do you think they do this?

2. Do you think your church ever slips into the erroneous concept of the omnicompetent pastor? If so, can anything be done about it?

3. How could it be that Peter Wagner suggests that the pastor of a local church might be effective even without the spiritual gift of pastor?

4. What is your view of the need for a local church to provide counseling services for its members? How effective are the church counseling services with which you are familiar?

5. Why would a combination of the gift of faith and the gift of leadership be important for the pastor of a growing church?

Notes

1. Warren H. Hartman, *Membership Trends: A Study of Decline and Growth in the United Methodist Church 1949-1975* (Nashville, TN: Discipleship Resources, 1976), p. 44.
2. United Presbyterian Church, *A Summary Report of the Committee on Membership Trends* (New York: 1976), p. 19.
3. Dan Martin, "The Church Growth Questions," *Home Missions* (December 1977), p. 12.
4. David A. Roozen, *Church Membership and Participation: Trends, Determinants and Implications for Policy and Planning* (Hartford, CT: Hartford Seminary Foundation, 1978), p. 58.
5. For a more thorough discussion of the celebration-congregation-cell concept, see C. Peter Wagner, *Your Church Can Grow* (Ventura, CA: Regal Books, 1976), pp. 97-109; and from a slightly different perspective, Lyle E. Schaller, *Assimilating New Members* (Nashville, TN: Abingdon Press, 1978), pp. 69-96.
6. Leslie B. Flynn, *Nineteen Gifts of the Spirit* (Wheaton, IL: Victor Books, 1974), p. 88.
7. Hartman, *Membership Trends*, p. 44.
8. Kenneth Cain Kinghorn, *Gifts of the Spirit* (Nashville, TN: Abingdon Press, 1976), p. 67.
9. Lyle E. Schaller, *Assimilating New Members* (Nashville, TN: Abingdon Press, 1978), p. 53.
10. Ray C. Stedman, *Body Life* (Ventura, CA: Regal Books, 1972), p. 79.

Chapter 7

THE EVANGELIST: THE PRIMARY ORGAN FOR GROWTH

Every separate bodily function has primary and secondary organs, which, working together, accomplish the task. Since this is true of the human body, I do not believe we stretch the apostle Paul's analogy of the physical body too far if we postulate that for given church functions, the Body of Christ has been provided with primary and secondary organs.

Take reproduction, for example. This is the physical function nearest to evangelism for the Church. Reproduction adds new members to the human race, and evangelism adds new members to the Body of Christ.

Obviously, the primary organ for accomplishing the task of human reproduction is the uterus. But when you think of it, the most perfect uterus God ever created could not reproduce if it were not for the simultaneous activity of the digestive system, the respiratory system, the endocrine system, the nervous system and the circulatory system. Although the uterus is the primary organ for reproduction, it is worthless without the healthy activity of the secondary organs.

SPIRITUAL REPRODUCTION

The application of reproduction to spiritual gifts is self-evident. The gift of evangelist is the primary organ that God has provided for reproduction. But the finest gift of evangelist in Christendom will not help churches grow if the other members of the Body, the secondary organs for church growth, are not also functioning in a healthy manner.

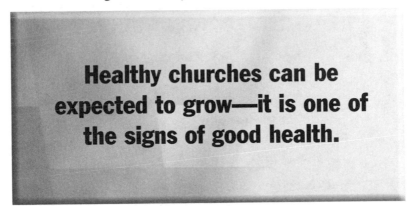

Healthy churches can be expected to grow—it is one of the signs of good health.

This brings us back to the observation we have made on many other occasions: Church growth and church health are interrelated. Only healthy bodies grow well, and only healthy churches grow well. Conversely, healthy churches can be expected to grow—it is one of the signs of good health. Statements such as "Our church is losing members, but we are healthy" do not square with all the biblical data about what God expects from the Body of Christ. One of the healthy church models we have in the New Testament is the Jerusalem church following Pentecost. Among other signs of good health, "the Lord added to the church daily those who were being saved" (Acts 2:47). If the Lord is not regularly adding new members, something is wrong with the church.

All church growth is not equally good growth. Although there are exceptions, the most beneficial kind of growth is conversion growth. That is what Acts 2:47 refers to. This is also called Kingdom growth, because new members are being brought into the kingdom of God. The gift of evangelist is only marginally necessary for *biological* growth, not necessary at all for *transfer* growth, but exceedingly important for *conversion* growth.

THE GIFT OF EVANGELIST

The gift of evangelist is mentioned in the gift list in Ephesians 4:11. In that context, as pointed out previously, it specifically refers to the office of evangelist. But in the same list, the prophet is presumed to have the gift of prophecy, the apostle the gift of apostle and the teacher the gift of teaching, so it does not seem to be far-fetched to suppose that the evangelist is presumed to have the spiritual gift of evangelist.

The gift of evangelist is the special ability that God gives to certain members of the Body of Christ to share the gospel with unbelievers in such a way that men and women become Jesus' disciples and responsible members of the Body of Christ.

The process of discovering the gift of evangelist is the same as for any other gift. Experiment, examine your feelings, evaluate your effectiveness and expect confirmation from the Body.

Desire and Results

One of our generation's outstanding evangelists, Leighton Ford, tells in his excellent book *Good News Is for Sharing* how he discovered his gift:

As a boy of sixteen, I first met Billy Graham and other gifted evangelists through the Youth for Christ movement. Observing these men and women in action, both personally and publicly, I felt something stirring within me. A longing to express my faith grew. Opportunities came to speak at youth groups and then at small evangelistic occasions. People were moved to accept Christ through what I said. While I believe God has given me certain other spiritual gifts, the gift of evangelism is primary.[1]

How Leighton Ford feels about his total spiritual life in light of what he recognizes as his primary gift is later expressed in these words: "I have discovered that it is only as I fan my gift into flame that I find fulfillment and growth in other areas of my Christian life."[2]

I like the advice that Pastor Rick Yohn gives to people in his church who are anxious to learn whether they have the gift of evangelist. He asks them two questions: (1) Do you have a strong desire to share your faith with others? I'm not asking whether you want to see people come to Christ. Most Christians want to see a life changed. But do you personally enjoy talking to others about Christ? (2) Are you seeing results?[3]

Varieties of the Gift

So far we have mentioned Leighton Ford and Billy Graham as well-known figures who have the gift of evangelist. We could add Reinhardt Bonnke or Luis Palau or Bill Bright. But they certainly are not to be considered as the only, or even the main, kind of person who has been given the gift. They are well known because they are full-time public professional evangelists, some of the very few as compared to the rest of the members of the Body of

Christ. Besides public evangelists, here are some of the other varieties that the gift of evangelist can assume:

1. Man or woman
2. Layperson or professional
3. Ordained or unordained
4. Full-time or part-time
5. Personal or public
6. Denominational or interdenominational
7. Monocultural or cross-cultural
8. Serving existing churches or planting new churches

The above list is certainly not exhaustive. One could think of Charles E. Fuller, who was not only a public evangelist but who also made particularly effective use of the medium of radio. Others are skilled in evangelizing through literature and music, as well as even basketball. God has provided a large variety of ways that the gift of evangelist can be ministered.

WHAT DOES EVANGELISM REALLY MEAN?

Regardless of how it is exercised, the objective of the gift of evangelist is the same: to bring unbelievers to a commitment to Jesus Christ and to each other in the Body of Christ.

This statement presupposes a certain definition of evangelism that is not fully accepted by all. This definition of evangelism is at odds with the *presence* definition so prevalent in the more liberal branches of Christianity. To presence people, evangelism is accomplished when a cup of cold water is given in the name of Jesus, whether or not the gospel is made clear to the recipient.

Neither is my definition satisfied with adding *proclamation* to presence, although many evangelicals hold tenaciously to that position. They argue that biblical evangelism is accomplished when the good news is faithfully proclaimed and understood, whether or not people become disciples of Jesus Christ.

The proclamation definition of evangelism does not include making disciples. Reported results from proclamation evangelism show only how many people heard the message and how many indicated a desire to make a decision for Christ.

A third definition, which I believe to be the most biblical one, warmly accepts the essential need for both presence and proclamation. But it maintains that the evangelistic process remains incomplete unless and until the person being evangelized has not only made a decision but has also proved that he or she is a disciple of Jesus by a visible commitment to the Body of Christ in some form or other. Some refer to this definition as the *persuasion* view.[4] This view regards people who have heard the gospel and rejected it, or who have not committed themselves to the Body of Christ as still unevangelized and as important targets for future evangelistic efforts.

Proclaiming the gospel does not necessarily require a spiritual gift, because salvation is so completely a work of the Holy Spirit. But proclaiming the gospel with unusual effectiveness so that regularly, week in and week out, new people come to faith in Christ and commitment to the Body, does require supernatural help through a spiritual gift.

HOW MANY HAVE THE GIFT OF EVANGELIST?

It goes without saying that not all members of the Body of Christ have the gift of evangelist. The whole body is not intended to be an eye (see 1 Cor. 12:17), much less a uterus. As I suggested in chapter 3, only a minority of the bodily members have been given any one gift. This in itself would narrow down the number who has the gift of evangelist to between 1 and 49 percent.

Of course, all the gifts are not evenly distributed. We have 2 eyes, 10 toes, 1 stomach and 32 teeth. That is why it would be foolish to figure that because there are 28 spiritual gifts, an average of 3.6 percent of the members of the Body would have any one gift. The spiritual organism is much more complex than that. But I find that the general tendency of Christians who are enthusiastic about getting certain tasks done in the Body is to carelessly overestimate how many of the members probably have one gift or another. If I want my particular job to get done well, I might tend to presume that an unrealistic number of people have the gift it takes. This happens very frequently with the gift of evangelist.

So far in this book, I have suggested only two figures for estimating the number of people who may have a certain gift. I said that those with the gift of intercession will probably figure to around 5 percent, and those with the gift of pastor will probably number between 3 and 6 percent, depending on some variables (see chapter 6).

I am much more secure in my present suggestion on the percentage for the gift of evangelist because, over a period of years, it has been tested in case after case and found to stand the test. The average Christian church can realistically expect that approximately 5 to 10 percent of its active adult members will have been given the gift of evangelist. A mounting quantity of empirical evidence indicates that if a church has as few as 5 percent of its active members mobilized for evangelism, a healthy growth pattern of more than 100 percent a decade is a realistic expectation. If God blesses a church by giving the gift of evangelist to 10 percent of its members, theoretically that church is in wonderful shape for growth.

CAN EVANGELISM BE OVEREMPHASIZED?

Evangelism is so important for church growth that one can understand why many Christian circles tend to overemphasize it. Overemphasize?

Before I answer this, I need to stress that I personally believe in evangelism so much so that I have dedicated my life to see that it happens on a worldwide scale. When I lived in California, my personalized license plate read "MT 28:19" and my wife's read "MT 28:20"—the Great Commission wherever we went. I have already suggested that the gift of evangelist is the primary organ in the Body of Christ for church growth. My objective in this book, as in every book I write, is to advance the evangelization of the world in our generation. I do not want to be misinterpreted on this matter in the slightest, because what I am about to say may be controversial.

To evangelize the world more effectively in our generation, I believe that many evangelicals need to get their heads out of the clouds concerning pronouncements about the degree of involvement the average Christian ought to have in active evangelistic work. We need to recognize certain basic things. For one thing, every true Christian should be in tune with God who is "not willing that any should perish but that all should come to repentance" (2 Pet. 3:9). Most every Christian desires to see people saved and brought into the fellowship of the Body. This is not the issue.

For another thing, every true Christian is a witness for Jesus Christ whether or not they have the gift of evangelist.

Furthermore, all Christians need to be prepared to share their faith with unbelievers and lead them to Christ whenever the opportunity presents itself. This is the Christian *role* that corresponds to this spiritual gift, which I will discuss in more detail shortly.

Having said this, it is time we admit that many good, faithful, consecrated, mature Christian people are in love with Jesus Christ, but they are not, do not care to be and, for all intents and purposes, will not be significantly involved in evangelization in any direct way. Indirectly, yes. They will contribute to the growth of the Body of Christ as the lungs, the small intestines, the kidneys and the thyroid gland contribute to human reproduction. And they will carry out their role of witness when circumstances so dictate. But they won't go around looking for new opportunities to share their faith.

It is a misunderstanding of biblical teaching, in my opinion, to try to convince all Christians that they have to be sharing the faith constantly as a part of their duty to the Master. We do not tell them that they have to teach all the time, pastor others all the time or be an apostle, a prophet, an administrator, a leader or a missionary, if they have not been given the spiritual equipment to do the job well. To make people feel guilty if they get gasoline and do not share Christ with the filling station attendant, if they do not leave tracts for the mail carrier or if they do not witness to the server in the restaurant may actually harm the Body of Christ more than help it.

A recent study was done of Conservative Baptist seminary students, who we can presume are representative of average or slightly above average Christians in their spiritual life and commitment, if perhaps somewhat lower in maturity. Certainly their honesty is commendable, given the excessive pressures that have been put on Christians to share their faith at all times. Of the sample studied, it was discovered that 10 percent of them share their faith once a week or more, and 10 percent of them have led one to three people to Christ within the past year. The other 90 percent, in varying degrees, indicated the following: (1) they have few contacts with non-Christians; (2) they do not desire help so they can relate better to non-Christians; (3) they probably would not bring unsaved friends to most church functions; (4) they do not want to learn to evangelize; (5) they feel they should lead people to Christ, but they do not want to give much time and energy to it; and (6) their prayer concern is high, but they do not spend much time actually praying for the unsaved.

Independent of this, but part of the same phenomenon, is a report from the Conservative Baptist Home Mission Board issued in June 1973, expressing concern that missionary candidates coming from the seminaries score high on the gifts of pastor and teacher, but low on the gift of evangelist.

How do we react to such a situation?

Some tend to throw up their hands, dress in sackcloth and ashes, figuratively speaking, and lament the low spiritual condition of our young people today. On the other hand, I tend to regard the situation as something that can and should be improved, but not something that is necessarily unhealthy.

WHO SHOULD FEEL GUILTY?

A key to relating the dynamic of the spiritual gift of evangelist to church growth lies in the question of the *location of guilt*. Guilt can be a blessing or it can be a curse, depending on where it is located.

First, Christians who have the gift of evangelist and who are not using their gift should be made to feel a responsibility for using it. If 5 percent actually have the gift, in probably the majority of churches that are plateaued or declining, only about .5 percent of the people are actually using the gift, if that many. This means that 4.5 percent of the people should rightly feel guilty if they are not evangelizing and evangelizing strenuously. Those who have the gift of exhortation should identify these people and help them discover, develop and use their gift. They will be happier and more fulfilled Christians, and the church will grow better. If this produces guilt, it will undoubtedly be a blessing.

Second, the 95 percent who have gifts other than that of evangelist should not be allowed to feel guilty if they assume secondary roles in the evangelistic process. This is where God intended them to be, or He would have given them the gift of evangelist. In some evangelical churches, the guilt-trip for not evangelizing is so severe that when the 5 percent do evangelize and bring new people into the church, the new converts are often turned off by what they find. The general tone of the body, the negative self-image of the members and the gloom and defeatism that can be felt in the atmosphere of the church make them think that everybody must have been baptized in vinegar! They quickly decide they want no part of such a crowd and soon vanish, unnoticed, out the back door.

PROJECTING
THE GIFT OF EVANGELIST

In light of what has been said, it is easily understood why the gift of evangelist is probably the most frequently projected of all the gifts.

In my experience, the most common technique used for projecting this gift by those who have it is to deny that they have it. Most American Christians who are aware of their ministry agree that two of our most outstanding Christian leaders who have the gift of evangelist are the late Bill Bright, founder of Campus Crusade for Christ, and James Kennedy, senior minister of Coral Ridge Presbyterian Church, Fort Lauderdale, Florida, and founder of Evangelism Explosion. They both have been personal friends of mine, and I have observed them carefully. My considered opinion is that they were both given the gift of evangelist, they developed it to a high degree, and they have used it for the glory of God and the growth of the Church. I have loved them both. I have loved spending time with them. I have loved hearing them tell of their experiences in sharing Christ and inspiring others to do the same. I publicly endorse the programs they developed as excellent methods for effective evangelism.

The reason I mention these two leaders, however, is that I have heard each of them specifically say that he does not have the gift of evangelist. For a long time I was haunted by the question Why would they deny such an obvious thing?

I know that they both would disagree with what I am saying. We have discussed spiritual gifts at length one-on-one, and both of them have expressed their belief that my hypothesis that 5 to 10 percent of the members of the Body of Christ have the gift of evangelist will be snatched up and used as a cop-out by Christians all over America. They have expressed that the notion that only those with the gift of evangelist ought to be evangelizing in a planned and structured way is erroneous, and that every Christian worth his or her spiritual salt ought to be using the Four Spiritual Laws regularly and be active in an Evangelism Explosion program or the equivalent of either. To them, the question is not gifts, but obedience.

Virtually every time I was with Bill Bright for more than 10 minutes at a time he told me moving stories of how God used him to lead people to Christ. Once he told me about a waitress in a restaurant in an Asian country who met Christ while he and his wife, Vonnette, were eating there. He told me about a hotel maid who prayed to receive Christ. He told me about several people seated next to him in airplanes whom he introduced to Jesus.

And here I am, an ordinary seminary professor who has the gift of teaching, completely at a loss to match him story for story. Who wants to hear about the outline for a new magazine article or a difficult concept simplified on a PowerPoint slide or a doctoral student who made a theoretical breakthrough in a Ph.D. dissertation or a new book just released by a faculty colleague or the 50 new students enrolled in a church growth seminar? If I were back in the days before I had come to terms with my own gift-mix, I might still be choked up with guilt when I hear these soul-winning stories and cannot respond by telling many of my own.

But no longer. Perhaps Bright and Kennedy would say, "I told you so. Wagner's copping out!" But here's what I do on an airplane.

Seeing an Airplane Seat as a Library

As I said previously, I believe that a Christian who knows his or her gift-mix ought to structure as much time as possible to use that gift or gifts. Whenever I get on an airplane, I consider myself in a library. For three or four or five uninterrupted hours, I have a beautiful chance to use one of my spiritual gifts. No telephone calls, no mail delivery, no knocks on the door. I take 8 to 12 pounds of reading material in my briefcase, because if, as a scholar, I am going to use my gift of knowledge, I must invest quality time reading large quantities of books, journals, magazines and newsletters, which I do voraciously. (See chapter 9 for an explanation of the gift of knowledge.)

If someone sits next to me, I make it a habit to pray and ask the Lord to keep that person quiet unless he or she has a heart that God has prepared for the gospel message at that moment. If so, I ask the Lord to open a conversation about Jesus. I have plenty of opportunities because people can tell I am a Christian immediately when they see what I am studying and see me say grace when the meal is served. When we do converse, the other person has usually figured out that I am a minister of some kind.

But more often than not, I do not converse with the person beside me because I am too busy using my spiritual gift. The Lord is not going to hold me responsible for what I do as an evangelist, but He is going to hold me responsible for what I do with my gift of knowledge. On the other hand, those who have the gift of evangelist should make every effort to converse with the people next to them on the plane and expect them to accept Christ before the next landing.

Understanding Rick Yohn's Frustrations

It is difficult for those who have a gift to understand the feelings of those who do not have it and who are thereby made to feel guilty. I have talked to several Campus Crusade staff members, for example, who suffer guilt feelings for not having the gift of evangelist but who feel that they are expected to show on their weekly reports that they are witnessing with the same effectiveness as other staff members who do have the gift. One person who has explained in writing how this has worked in his life is Rick Yohn, author of an outstanding book on spiritual gifts.

Rick Yohn tells about the frustrations that plagued him while he worked on the Campus Crusade staff. "I would hear about other staff workers introducing students to Christ," he writes, "and I would compare their results with mine. They always saw greater numerical results." This bothered Rick deeply, and he searched his heart before God. "Was I lacking faith?" he would ask. He honestly did not believe so. Some people did respond to his efforts, but not many. Then he asked, "Was my message deficient?" The answer to that question obviously was no, because he used the same Four Spiritual Laws that the more successful staff members were using.

At that point Yohn had to conclude, "Either I am a complete failure as a minister or my gifts are in an area other than evangelism." He found that his basic gift-mix was pastor-teacher, and he has enjoyed ministering his gift for the glory of God ever since. Although he has served in several pastorates since leaving Campus Crusade, he still sees few new people come to Christ directly through his ministry. But he is liberated. He now thinks it is a shame when spirituality is judged on the basis of how many souls a person has won.[5]

I myself consciously try to avoid gift projection. I would not want to judge the spirituality of other Christians on the basis of whether they had a Ph.D. or whether they had become fluent in the vernacular of a second culture, qualities that my gifts of knowledge and missionary require of me. I try not to get disturbed when I see some people teach and know that they are not communicating well with the listeners. I try not to be disdainful if someone I am conversing with does not understand the meaning of "ethnotheology," "homogeneity," "centered set theory," "assimilationist racism," "the excluded middle," "spiritual mapping" or "dynamic equivalence." They have not been reading and studying the books I have been studying. If I did engage in such gift projection, I might suspect that I was not obeying the Golden Rule, because I was not doing to others as I would have them do to me.

IS THIS A COP-OUT?

I agree with Leighton Ford, an evangelist who is willing to recognize his own evangelistic gift. Although Leighton admits that
God makes certain people evangelists through spiritual gifts, he
also says, "We must not use the teaching of spiritual gifts as a
cop-out to avoid our responsibility to share Christ with others.
You may not be called as an evangelist, but you and every
Christian, by an attitude of love, by compassionate concern, and
by well-chosen words, can have the privilege to lead others . . .
toward Jesus Christ."[6] This is timely advice.

Leighton Ford refers here to what we have been calling the
Christian *role*. Every Christian is called to be a faithful witness of
Jesus Christ. David Hubbard, who was president of Fuller
Seminary for 30 years, explains it this way:

> Not all of us have the gift of evangelism. I admire people
> who can lead others to Jesus Christ right on the spot,
> who have the ability to turn every conversation into an
> occasion for sharing God's plan of salvation. I am not
> one of those, but I have a story to share—and so do you.
> I have a relationship with Christ that I can describe—and
> so do you. Evangelism will best take place when all
> of God's people have learned to express their winsome
> witness.[7]

I have found this to be true in my life. For example, I led my
daughter's husband and his mother to Christ. A couple came to
clean our house and they both accepted Christ. I recently spent a
few days in the hospital and found that my roommate's illness
was life threatening. I witnessed to him and he was born again. He
soon died, and his widow wrote me a long letter telling how her
husband's life had been totally changed. I give these examples, not

to show how heroic I am, because occasions like this are few and far between in my ministry. Just the opposite is true. I give God the glory for allowing a person like me, who obviously does not have the gift of evangelist, to be effective in my role as a witness from time to time.

My role as a Christian is to be a witness for my Lord at any time, and I am delighted when God gives me the opportunity. But I have found that whenever I force it, I tend to blow it. So I let God do it for me.

Whoever uses his or her lack of having the spiritual gift of evangelist as a cop-out from witnessing displeases God. But whoever insists that another person divert valuable energy that could be used for exercising their spiritual gifts into unproductively attempting to force them to concentrate on a weak role likewise displeases God.

CATALYZING NEW CONVERTS FOR EFFECTIVE WITNESS

Contrary to what some people would expect, the more mature a Christian becomes in the faith, the less potential that person has as an effective witness. The main reason for this is that an increasing involvement with the Body of Christ over a period of time steadily reduces the number of contacts a person has with unbelievers. Before a person becomes a Christian, all of his or her friends and relatives may be non-Christians. The same is true for new converts before they become well assimilated into the family of God. After a person becomes a Christian, the possibilities to use the role of witness are usually high—but only for a limited period of time.

If the role of witness is ever to be structured for church growth, here is the area for major concentration. New

Christians, before they may be mature enough to discover what their spiritual gifts are, should be encouraged by every means to use their remaining contacts with unsaved friends and relatives for evangelistic purposes. But in most cases they will not know how to lead others to Christ too well. Chances are, at least 9 out of 10 have not been given the gift of evangelist. It seems to me, therefore, that the strongest kind of mobilization for evangelism in a church is to link up these 5 to 10 percent of the mature Christians who do have the *gift* of evangelist with the new converts who have a *role* of witness and to introduce their friends and relatives to Jesus Christ through this kind of teamwork.

This happened in a church in California some time ago when Doris and I were members of what was known as the Voyagers Sunday School class. One of the members of the class, Steve Lazarian, had the gift of evangelist along with his wife, Iris. He owned an electrical contracting business. They met a man also in the electrical business who had been transferred to California from back East, and they led him to the Lord. He then witnessed the best way he could to his wife and to the people at his office. Soon he brought a woman from his office to class, then she brought a friend of hers, and then the man's wife became interested. He got all three together with the Lazarians, and the Lazarians led them to Christ. In six months, the Voyagers grew six percent, a good growth rate for any congregation.

For this dynamic to operate smoothly, of course, a steady supply of new converts is needed in the church. Some churches, however, do not like new converts too much, and they telegraph their attitude in subtle ways. New converts are something like babies around the house—a nuisance, when it comes right down to it. But like babies, they are nuisances that should be loved and nurtured. They should not be expected to behave like mature

Christians, but if they are made to feel welcome and cared for in every way, they will quickly mature. Before they do, however, their role of witness and their contacts with unbelievers should be cultivated with diligence. Churches that know how to do this usually grow well.

REFLECTIONS

1. Why do people say that conversion growth is the most important kind of church growth? Do you see much of that in your church? If not, what could be done about it?
2. Some people feel guilty because they do not evangelize enough. In which cases is guilt an appropriate response? In which other cases is guilt inappropriate?
3. In chapter 2, we explained the concept of gift projection. Can you give examples of people who tend to project their gift of evangelist on others?
4. All believers who do not have the gift of evangelist do have a role of witness. How do you think this should work out in practice?
5. Overall, would you consider it wise to stress that only five percent of Christians have the gift of evangelist? Why or why not?

Notes

1. Leighton Ford, *Good News Is for Sharing* (Elgin, IL: David C. Cook Publishing Company, 1977), p. 83.
2. Ibid.
3. Rick Yohn, *Discover Your Spiritual Gift and Use It* (Wheaton, IL: Tyndale House Publishers, 1974), p. 64.

4. The presence-proclamation-persuasion discussion is further developed in C. Peter Wagner, *Strategies for Church Growth* (Ventura, CA: Regal Books, 1987), pp. 117-130.

5. Yohn, *Discover Your Spiritual Gift and Use It*, p. 64.

6. Ford, *Good News Is for Sharing*, p. 83.

7. David Allan Hubbard, "A Winsome Witness," *Today's Christian* (September 1978), p. 2.

Chapter 8

UNDERSTANDING THE
MISSIONARY GIFT

Some books on church growth are written as though the expansion of the local church were the only important kind of growth. It certainly is important and undoubtedly is the kind of growth in which pastors of churches and lay leaders are most immediately and intensely interested. Local church growth is strongly emphasized in this book, but I would not consider the book complete if it did not include at least one chapter dealing with the vast number of people outside the normal reach of the evangelistic program of a local church. The spiritual gift that most directly relates to this is the gift of missionary.

FOUR KINDS OF CHURCH GROWTH

Church growth theory discerns four basic kinds of growth.

Internal Growth. Internal growth is the spiritual growth of Christians who are already members of the Body of Christ. Through it, they learn to love God more deeply, worship more intensely, pray more fervently, witness more effectively, care for each other more lovingly, study God's Word more intelligently and exhibit other Christian graces that reflect Christian maturity. Internal growth is a prerequisite to other kinds of growth, because mature Christians are the instruments God uses for reaching others for Christ and folding them into the fellowship of believers.

Expansion Growth. Expansion growth is the growth of the local congregation through membership. It is the kind I previously referred to as the chief concern of most pastors.

Extension Growth. Extension growth is growth through planting new churches. Unfortunately, extension growth has been one of the most severely neglected areas for effective evangelism in America. Compared to expansion growth, extension growth is a much more efficient and cost-effective way to evangelize the unchurched, including the "Christian" country of America. I have no doubt in my mind that simply by launching an aggressive program of new church planting, almost any denomination in America could reverse the trend of church membership decline that has been plaguing many of them.

Bridging Growth. Bridging growth is also growth through planting new churches, but in bridging growth the new churches are planted in a different culture. Extension growth is planting new churches among "our kind of people." Bridging growth is planting churches among other kinds of people who could not reasonably be expected to be folded into the fellowship of our particular local church or who simply prefer to worship God in ways different from the way we do it. Bridging growth is (1) the top priority for completing the task of world evangelization and (2) uniquely dependent upon the missionary gift. But before we go into this, I want to explain one more set of concepts.

FOUR KINDS OF EVANGELISM

All evangelism is not the same. In the preceding chapter, we mentioned the gift of evangelist and the many different variations within which that gift can be exercised. Here are some further variations that bring the cultural aspect to bear.

E-1 Evangelism. E-1 evangelism is monocultural. It is the shorthand term that refers to winning those of your own culture to Jesus Christ and assumes that the new converts will feel at home in your own kind of local church. It includes both expansion and extension growth.

E-2 and E-3 Evangelism. Both E-2 and E-3 are cross-cultural. They are actually subdivisions of bridging growth. E-2 is evangelization in cultures different from the culture of the evangelist, but only slightly different. E-3 is evangelism in vastly different cultures. The difference between the two is in degree, not in kind, because they both involve starting churches in different cultures. Note that geographical distances have nothing to do with this. People at an E-3 distance can often be found in the same city or in the same neighborhood.

E-0 Evangelism. To complete the picture, E-0 evangelism means winning people to Christ who are already church members. Some churches in America have many members who are not born-again or committed to Christ; they obviously need to be evangelized.

THE UNREACHED PEOPLES

This book emphasizes the growth of the church. Most of the content deals with E-1 *expansion* growth. But this chapter focuses on E-2 and E-3 *bridging* growth. Thus, it addresses itself to the challenge of the unreached peoples, those thousands of millions of people in the world who have not yet heard of Jesus Christ and who need someone from outside their own culture to bring them the good news if they are ever going to hear it.

Those interested in total fulfillment of the Great Commission need to see the whole picture. No one has done more consistent and thorough research on this than Ralph Winter of the U.S. Center for World Mission. He addressed the 1974 International Congress on World Evangelization at Lausanne, Switzerland, on the subject "The Highest Priority: Cross-Cultural Evangelism," bringing world attention to this tremendous need.[1] Winter's organization, although admitting the need for E-0 and E-1 evangelism, nevertheless has dedicated all its resources to E-2 and E-3 evangelism. From Winter, we learn that for the purposes of evangelization, the world can be divided statistically into four categories:

1. *Active Christians are people who have been truly born again or who are committed to Christ.* These people are responsible members of local churches, who believe the Bible and who take seriously its command to make disciples of all nations.

2. *Inactive Christians would answer "Christian" if asked what their religion is on a world census.* But most of them are Christian in name only. They are not committed to sharing their faith in any way with others. They provide little support for evangelization.

3. *Culturally near non-Christians do not yet know Jesus Christ.* Their culture has a viable Christian church and they can likely be reached by E-1 evangelism. Sometimes they might be far removed from other Christians of their own kind of people *geographically*, but culturally they are near neighbors.

4. *Culturally distant non-Christians are people who are part of a culture into which Christianity has not yet penetrated.* They are the unreached peoples. The only way they can be reached is by E-2 and E-3 cross-cultural

evangelism. The most surprising thing about these
unreached people groups is not so much that they
are there, but that there are so many of them. In
fact, some missiological researchers calculate that
one-third of the world's population will not be
reached for Christ without cross-cultural evangelism. Little wonder they are considered the highest
priority.

The most difficult kind of evangelism, quite obviously, is E-
3, and the second most difficult is E-2. E-1 extension growth
(starting new churches in the same culture) is the next most difficult, and E-1 expansion is the easiest. This is one reason that,
unless cross-cultural evangelism intentionally is made a high
priority, E-1 tends to take the front seat, and the extremely
important E-2 and E-3 tragically become items far down the
agenda.

The greatest challenge for cross-cultural evangelism is, of
course, what we usually think of as the foreign mission field. The
largest numbers of unreached peoples are found among
Chinese, Hindus, Muslims and Buddhists—in that order. But
this should not blind us to the great need for E-2 and E-3 evangelistic work right here in the United States.

People Blindness and Its Cure

Many people do not recognize unreached peoples because they
are people-blind. People blindness is the malady that prevents us
from seeing groups of people around us who are not able to hear
the message of the gospel or to respond to it in the ways we tend
to express it. Those of us who are people-blind think that our
church is good enough for everyone and that our doors are open

to all. If some people do not happen to like what they find in our church, we consider it *their* problem, not *ours*. We think all Christians should talk the same language, worship alike, enjoy the same kind of music, have their services at the same time and for the same length, and form close friendships with people from various kinds of groups.

> **Those of us who are people-blind think that our church is good enough for everyone and that our doors are open to all.**

The fact of the matter is that churches do not grow that way. Throughout history, Christian churches have normally grown among just one kind of people through E-1 evangelism. Congregational life is attractive to unbelievers when they see people in those congregations with whom they can feel at home. If they cannot feel at home, due to language and cultural differences, they will best be won to Christ through E-2 or E-3 evangelism. This means starting new churches that from the beginning will be *their* kind of churches, not *our* kind of churches. Foreign missionaries know this principle of church growth, but some of us Americans find it harder to apply in our own country. We suffer from people blindness partially as a result of our embarrassment over racism, discrimination and social injustices that have been perpetrated throughout United States history by the dominant Anglo-Americans.

"Unmelted" Americans

The first mainline denomination in the United States to understand this form of church growth and to concentrate heavily on
the principles of E-2 and E-3 evangelism was the Southern
Baptist Convention. The convention's North American Mission
Board in Atlanta, Georgia, particularly when it was under the
leadership of Oscar Romo, director of the Language Missions
Department, began to lead the way. Southern Baptists have been
far ahead of most other denominations in perceiving the true
spiritual need of Americans who are unmelted, so to speak, and
in planting among them something different from the ordinary
Southern Baptist Anglo-American church.

Southern Baptist leader Oscar Romo maintains that all
churches, like it or not, are cultural, ethnic or subculture group-
ings. He philosophizes, "Our job is to evangelize, not to assimi-
late. People go to church because they want to. If they don't want
to, they won't go. You go where you feel comfortable."[2]

Recognizing the need for cross-cultural sensitivity among
Christians, Romo goes on to say, "To reach people, we must be
aware of cultural units and cultural differences. There has to be
room for the gospel to penetrate a given group without necessarily changing that group's background. It changes their sense
of values, but you still end up having subcultures."[3]

How the Gospel Spreads

The three most important incidents for spreading the gospel in
the New Testament after Jesus' ascension were (1) the bridge
from Hebrew Jews to Hellenistic Jews (see Acts 2), (2) the
bridge from Jews to Samaritans (see Acts 8), and (3) the bridge
from Jews to Gentiles (see Acts 11). They were all cross-cultural
E-2 and E-3 situations.

This is true today also. The most significant events in world evangelization occur when the gospel takes permanent root in a new culture, among an unreached people.

THE GIFT OF MISSIONARY

The reason I have spent so much time dealing with the world picture is that cross-cultural evangelism is uniquely dependent upon the spiritual gift of missionary. This is a hidden gift for hidden people. I call it a hidden gift because hardly any other book on spiritual gifts that I have found discusses it or acknowledges it as a gift. One reason for this might be that in the Bible the gift of missionary is not as explicitly described as a spiritual gift as most of the others; however, in Ephesians 3:6-8 this gift appears, which is evident once the passage is explained.

The gift of missionary is the special ability that God gives to certain members of the Body of Christ to minister whatever other spiritual gifts they have in a second culture.

Most Christians, as are most human beings, are monocultural. They are born and raised and marry and die among only one kind of people. Their culture enables them to interact with, behave like and understand others around them, without any special training other than the process of socialization, which all humans go through at an early age. They may, of course, come into contact with other cultures from time to time. They may travel abroad and enjoy seeing other kinds of people. They may live in a city in the United States where housing, schools and employment are integrated and where contact with people from other cultures is part of daily life. They may also have close friends with people from another culture. They may have made the effort to learn a foreign language. All this and, when it comes right down to it, most people still are monocultural.

People who have the gift of missionary not only enjoy coming into contact with other cultures but also go through a second process of socialization called acculturation. They enjoy the challenge of living in another culture while cutting ties with their first culture on a long-term basis. When they do, they initially suffer their share of culture shock, but they recover rapidly. They may be attacked by Montezuma's revenge, but they eventually become immune to the new bugs in the food and drink of another people. They learn the language more rapidly than those who do not have the gift. They quickly pick up slang words, tones of voice and body language not described in textbooks. They feel at home with people of the second culture. And most of all, they are eventually accepted by the others as "one of us."

Although intercultural contact is enriching for every person, God does not expect every Christian to identify with a second culture. He gives the gift of missionary only to some. In the United States, the last I checked, out of about 50 million active Christian adults, some 40,000 were serving as missionaries. This is less than one-tenth of one percent! The research I have been able to do points to something like a maximum of one percent of the Body of Christ who would have the missionary gift.

PROJECTING
THE GIFT OF MISSIONARY

The gift of missionary is another one of those gifts that is frequently projected. Time and again I hear some enthusiastic preacher say, "Every Christian is a missionary!" The doctrine of spiritual gifts tells us that this is a ridiculous statement if "missionary" is understood in its true sense. In most cases, however, I do not think they are referring to specialized E-2 and E-3 evangelism. They probably have never realized that there is such a thing as a missionary gift. What they probably are trying to say is, "Every Christian is a witness," with which I heartily concur.

In reality, it could be counterproductive to encourage anyone and everyone to volunteer to be a cross-cultural missionary. Sad to say, some missionaries have been on the field for 30 years, although in reality they never had the gift in the first place. Both their home church and the mission field probably would have been better off if they had stayed home. The mission field is something like the Marine Corps: God needs a few choice (gifted) men and women. If any place in God's work requires a high degree of aptitude, training and competence, it is in the cross-cultural task of reaching the unreached peoples. I do not believe it is helpful to give an appeal at a missionary conference that says, "You must go to the field unless God calls you to stay home!" It would be much better to focus the appeal on discovering spiritual gifts and having a positive call to go to the mission field.

GIFT CONFUSION

Sometimes the gift of missionary is confused with the gift of evangelist. It should be evident, however, that some evangelists have the missionary gift and some do not. Those who do have the gift of missionary should evangelize in another culture (as well as in their own), but those who do not have the gift should concentrate on a monocultural ministry. They will be effective in E-1 evangelism, but not in the more demanding E-2 and E-3 evangelism.

Another major area of confusion that often arises is between the missionary gift and that of apostle. Before we contrast the two, let's first look at the gift of apostle.

THE GIFT OF **APOSTLE**

Although I love *The Living Bible*, I regret that it frequently translates the Greek *apostolos* (apostle) as "missionary." This tends to cloud the important distinction between the gift of missionary and the gift of apostle.

The biblical evidence strongly supports the continuity of the gift of apostle. The original 12 apostles have a unique place in Christian history and they will be commemorated permanently in the foundation of the New Jerusalem (see Rev. 21:14), but they were not the only apostles. First Corinthians 15 mentions that after the resurrection, Jesus appeared to "the twelve" and then also to "all the apostles," indicating that there were apostles other than the Twelve (vv. 5,7). Furthermore, the warnings against false apostles would be nonsense if apostles were limited to the Twelve (see 2 Cor. 11:13; Rev. 2:2).

Several, other than the Twelve, are mentioned by name as apostles. They include Matthias (see Acts 1:26), Barnabas (see Acts 14:14), Paul (see Rom. 1:1), Andronicus and Junia (see Rom. 16:7), Timothy and Silas (see 1 Thess. 1:1; 2:6), and others. In New Testament times, there undoubtedly were many apostles who were not named in the Bible. Through the ages, as well as today, many of God's gifted servants have been, and are, true apostles.

The gift of apostle is the special ability that God gives to certain members of the Body of Christ to assume and to exercise divinely imparted authority in order to establish the foundational government of an assigned sphere of ministry within the

Church. An apostle hears from the Holy Spirit and sets things in order accordingly for the Church's health, growth, maturity and outreach.

The New Apostolic Reformation, which I referred to in the introduction, has brought about the most radical change in the way of doing church since the Protestant Reformation.[4] Of the many specific changes that the church is currently experiencing, the most radical of them all is *the amount of spiritual authority delegated by the Holy Spirit to individuals.* The two operative words in this statement are "authority" and "individuals."

Traditionally, the assumption in churches across the board has been that final authority always rests in the hands of groups, not individuals. We have become comfortable with terms such as "church boards," "sessions," "congregational meetings," "synods," "presbyteries," "councils of bishops," "general assemblies," "state conventions" and any number of similar entities, all designed to reflect the principle that no individual should be entrusted with final decisions in church life.

This is no longer true of churches that have chosen to align themselves with what God is doing in this Second Apostolic Age, which I date as beginning in 2001. Church leadership and final authority is now much more in the hands of individuals than it has been for 1,800 years or more. This plays out mainly through the gift of leadership (not the gift of pastor), exercised by pastors of local churches, and through the gift of apostle, exercised translocally.

Gift Versus Office

Let's keep in mind the important difference between the *gift* of apostle and the *office* of apostle. The gift is received by grace, while the office is received by works. God is the only One who gives the gifts and decides who is to have them. We do not earn them; we receive them by grace. That is why, as I have explained, the biblical word for spiritual gift, "charisma," contains "charis," the Greek word for "grace."

However, God does not confer the office of apostle—people do. Those who truly have the gift will naturally exhibit the fruit of that gift. "By their fruits you will know them" (Matt. 7:20). When peer-level leaders recognize the fruit of apostle in an individual's life and ministry, they are then in a position to confer the office, which they do through ordination or commissioning. The demeaning phrase "self-appointed apostle" does not describe any who truly have the gift and the office of apostle.

Vertical Apostles and Horizontal Apostles

Not all apostles are alike. The two major kinds of apostle are vertical apostles and horizontal apostles.

When most people hear the word "apostle," they first think of vertical apostles, apostles who oversee a number of churches and ministries comprising an apostolic network. Apostle Paul would be a biblical example. Vertical apostles provide ongoing spiritual covering to pastors and other leaders in their networks. The majority of apostles are vertical apostles.

On the other hand, horizontal apostles are primarily conveners. God has given them the gift to call others together at specific times for specific purposes. Apostle James, who called the Council of Jerusalem, would be a biblical example. While Peter and Paul, for example, were in the Council meetings, they were under James's authority. But when they left Jerusalem, James did not continue to oversee the ministries of Peter, Paul or the other apostles who attended. He was a horizontal apostle.

Spheres of Authority

Apostles, as we see in the definition of the gift of apostle, have been entrusted with tremendous authority. They have authority over individual leaders, over churches, over networks of churches and over ministries. Apostles are those most likely to hear and declare what the Spirit is saying to the churches (see Rev. 2:7). Because of this, the office of apostle is frequently misunderstood as being dictatorial, self-serving or empire building. Anointed apostles, however, do not abuse the authority they have. They are not autocratic. They build and work closely with leadership teams. They draw heavily on the wisdom of other leaders, as well as team with prophets and intercessors.

It is important to keep in mind that apostolic authority is only applicable within the sphere or spheres that God has assigned. For example, when the apostle Paul wrote to the Corinthians, he found it necessary to assert his apostolic authority in 1 Corinthians 9:1. He then went on to say, "If I am not an apostle to others, yet doubtless I am to you" (v. 2). Paul recognized that he did not have apostolic authority over all the churches everywhere, but he affirmed that his God-assigned apostolic sphere definitely included the church at Corinth. In 2 Corinthians 10:8, he said that he would "boast" about his authority, and then went on to say, "We, however, will not boast beyond measure, but within the limits of the *sphere* which God appointed us—a sphere which especially includes you" (v. 13).

Apostles by Other Names

Today, many titles are given to those who are assigned responsibility over a number of churches. Depending on the denomination, they can be called bishops, district superintendents, overseers, moderators, conference ministers, presidents, executive secretaries or a number of other titles. Theoretically, all of these people should be selected for their position because their spiritual gift of apostle has been recognized by the Body of Christ. It is no secret, however, that in practice many, if not most, unfortunately have been elevated to their position on the basis of seniority, prestige, personality or politics. This soon becomes evident by the kind of leadership mode they tend to assume. To borrow sociological terms, top-ranking church leaders may fall into one of two kinds of leadership categories:

1. *Rational-Legal Leaders.* Their authority comes from their position, not from their person. They are obeyed, sometimes grudgingly, because of the office they represent, not because of their gift. They are often gloomy, irascible, pessimistic and insecure. They are easily threatened by up-and-coming new leadership.

2. *Charismatic Leaders.* Their authority is derived from a God-given gift. Others obey them because they want to, not because they are forced to. These leaders constantly add value to their followers. Their leadership does not depend on the office or the title, even though both the office and the title are important. They are usually easygoing, unthreatened, optimistic and pleasant to be around. I believe this is God's mode for true apostolic leadership.

CONTEMPORARY APOSTLES

Some years ago, when I first began recognizing the contemporary gift of apostle, I came into contact with Pastor Chuck Smith of Calvary Chapel in Costa Mesa, California. When he led this church in the late 1960s, during the Jesus People Movement, he ministered to approximately 25,000 people every week. It was one of the largest and fastest-growing churches in America.

Not only was Chuck Smith the pastor of the mother church, but his leadership had also encouraged at least 450 other Calvary Chapel churches to be planted throughout the country. At the time, it was reported that of the 15 fastest-growing congregations in the United States, no fewer than five of them were Calvary Chapel.

Although he himself is uncomfortable in accepting the title of apostle, I have cited these statistics to argue that Chuck Smith does indeed have the gift of apostle. The growth of churches in our generation has been catalyzed by the apostolic gift that God has given to Chuck Smith, just as surely as the growth of the churches in first-century Asia Minor was catalyzed by Paul's apostolic gift.

Chuck Smith well fits the pattern of the charismatic leader, which I just described. A newspaper story on Calvary Chapel once characterized him as "a balding, ebullient Bible teacher who radiates good health and friendly, open cheerfulness which attracts crowds of enthusiastic believers and followers."[5] But while this is true, it is not the whole picture. I also have been told that among peers in the leadership positions in the various Calvary Chapel churches, Chuck Smith's "soft" words carry incredible authority. When he speaks what he feels to be God's will, he says it quietly, he says it only once, and he expects it to be obeyed. It usually is.

Some may wonder how many apostles there may be in the Body of Christ. In proportion to the whole, we would not expect very many. I would guess perhaps 1 in 5,000 or 1 in 10,000, although I may well be wrong. At this writing, the number of identifiable apostles is on the rise, but mainly because many who have been given the gift of apostle are just now beginning to accept the office of apostle for the first time. I currently have the privilege of serving as the presiding apostle of the International Coalition of Apostles, which embraces 380 apostles, but I expect organizations like this to multiply throughout the world in the years to come.

PAUL, THE MISSIONARY

Paul not only had the gift of apostle, but he also had the gift of missionary. He was a cross-cultural worker and he constantly perceived himself in that role. Ephesians 3 is the main Scripture passage on the gift of missionary. There Paul speaks of his special ability, as a Jew, to carry the gospel to the Gentiles. Paul was "a Pharisee, the son of a Pharisee" (Acts 23:6), a Hebrew "brought up . . . at the feet of Gamaliel" (22:3), and a recipient of the legacy of prejudice and disdain that most Jews had for Gentiles in the first century. I remember reading one commentator who speculated that the only prejudice barrier in today's world that even approaches the feeling of first-century Jews for Gentiles is the prejudice that Brahmins have for untouchables in India. For a Jew to reach Gentiles effectively then, supernatural help was definitely needed.

Paul says that his ability to communicate to Gentiles that they should be members of the Body of Christ just as the Jews were was due to the "gift of grace" that God had given him (Eph. 3:7). This is a clear reference to a spiritual gift, which I have chosen to call the gift of missionary, although that label itself is not used in the Bible. But if Paul's gift was cross-cultural communication, which is indicated here, "missionary" seems to fit the concept well.

In each one of the three accounts of Paul's conversion in the book of Acts, the gift of missionary is implied. For example,

Ananias of Damascus, the man God used to speak to Paul and to restore his sight after Paul's life-changing experience on the Damascus Road, heard these words about Paul from God Himself: "He is a chosen vessel of Mine to bear My name before Gentiles" (Acts 9:15). So consistently did Paul live out his specific calling to minister to the Gentiles that he defended their point of view in the Jerusalem Council (see 15), and he ultimately was arrested and imprisoned because the Jews thought he had turned traitor and betrayed them (see 21:28-29).

Paul described what the missionary gift looked like to him. He mentioned that he could become a Jew to the Jews and a Gentile ("without law") to the Gentiles. "I have become all things to all men," he said, "that I might by all means save some" (1 Cor. 9:22). Successful cross-cultural workers today exhibit the same qualities. It is relatively easy for them to identify with and fit into other cultures because God so enables them with the gift of missionary.

PAUL, PETER AND JAMES, THE APOSTLES

Both Paul and Peter had the gift of apostle and were so recognized by the churches. But Paul also had the gift of missionary and Peter did not. Paul was a cross-cultural apostle while Peter was a monocultural apostle. Peter, it is true, had some cross-cultural experiences. He was the one chosen to present the gospel to the Gentiles in the house of Cornelius, although it seemed to be an extremely difficult experience for him. He later visited the Gentile churches in Antioch, but when the crunch came, he refused to eat with Gentiles and thus infuriated his friend Paul. Paul chose to tell, in his epistle to the Galatians, how he withstood Peter to his face in Antioch (see 2:11). Paul then, once and for all, clarified that he was an apostle to the Gentiles ("the uncircumcised," v. 7), but Peter was an apostle to the Jews ("the circumcised," v. 8). These were clearly defined spheres. Peter had a difficult time in cross-cultural situations, mainly because he did not have the missionary gift that Paul had.

Not only Peter, but James and John also recognized that they were apostles who did not have the missionary gift. This is described in Galatians 2:9 where James, Peter and John recognized that Paul had a special "grace" (the root word for "charisma" is used here); thereby, Paul and Barnabas should do the cross-cultural work among Gentiles while the other three remained in monocultural work among Jews.

THE ROLE OF WORLD CHRISTIAN

Let's go back for a moment to the difference between a spiritual gift and a Christian role.

Although only a few people may have the gift of missionary and, thereby, would be expected to minister in a second culture, all Christians have a role of supporting God's program to "make disciples of all the nations" (Matt. 28:19) in every way possible. I like the term now being used to designate people who in one way or another have become informed about the cause of world evangelization and who are supporting it in whatever way they can. The exercise of their role is above average. They are called World Christians. World Christians may have a variety of other spiritual gifts, but they have decided to use whatever gifts they have in ways that specifically further the cause of reaching the unreached.

Experimenting with the missionary gift is more possible today than ever before. Increasing numbers of the missionary force of North American missionaries are short-term workers who sign up for a few months to a few years for some specialized job. If these short-term workers do this in prayer and with the expectation that, through the experience, God will indicate clearly whether they have the missionary gift and whether cross-cultural work should possibly become a career, those who find that they do not have the gift per se can still join the ranks of World Christians.

REFLECTIONS

1. Do you think that more cross-cultural evangelism is needed in your city or community? If so, name some specific groups that are not being evangelized well.
2. Discuss the concept of people blindness along with the popular myth that America is a melting pot. How might these ideas hinder true evangelism?
3. Why is it inaccurate to say, "Every Christian is a missionary"?
4. Try to explain the difference between the gift of missionary and the gift of apostle.
5. Do you agree that the gift of apostle is present in the Body of Christ today? Give your reasons.

Notes

1. Ralph D. Winter, "The Highest Priority: Cross-Cultural Evangelism," *Let the Earth Hear His Voice*, ed. J. D. Douglas (Minneapolis, MN: World Wide Publications, 1975), pp. 213-258.
2. Oscar Romo, quoted in Dan Martin, "The Church-Growth Question," *Home Missions* (December 1977), p. 19.
3. Ibid.
4. For details on the New Apostolic Reformation, see my books *The New Apostolic Churches* (Ventura, CA: Regal Books, 1998), *Churchquake!* (Ventura, CA: Regal Books, 1999) and *Changing Church* (Ventura, CA: Regal Books, 2004).
5. George Grey, "Calvary Chapels Sprouting Like Mushrooms Over U.S.," *The Register* (March 26, 1978), p. 1.

THE REST OF THE BODY

Up to this point, 18 spiritual gifts have been defined and discussed. Of them, the primary gift for total world evangelization was identified as the gift of missionary. The primary gift for local church growth is the gift of evangelist. The primary gift for the total health of the local church is the gift of pastor. These three gifts—pastor, evangelist and missionary—are so crucial for church growth that each required a whole chapter. The other 15 were presented and discussed either as they related to the three major gifts or as they illustrated some general principle of spiritual gifts.

In this chapter, I will explain the remaining 10 gifts. I need to state once again that they are not secondary to the health of the Body of Christ any more than the ears, the tongue, the lungs and the skin are secondary to bodily health in general. But they are secondary to the *reproductive* function in both cases. Therefore, because this book is stressing the relationship of spiritual gifts to the growth of the local church, these other 10 gifts will be discussed a bit more briefly.

THE GIFTS OF
KNOWLEDGE AND WISDOM

Although the twin gifts of wisdom and knowledge are mentioned in that order in 1 Corinthians 12, I am reversing the order here because I want to discuss them in sequence. Knowledge relates to the discovery of truth and wisdom deals with the application of truth to life.

I like Ralph Neighbour's medical analogy to explain the difference between the gift of knowledge and the gift of wisdom.[1] The person who has the gift of knowledge is equivalent to the medical researcher who gains new insights into physiology, genetics or vaccines. The person who has the gift of wisdom is equivalent to the physician who has the ability to diagnose the patient's problem and to apply the resources of medical science to that particular case.

THE GIFT OF KNOWLEDGE

The gift of knowledge is the special ability that God gives to certain members of the Body of Christ to discover, accumulate, analyze and clarify information and ideas that are pertinent to the growth and well-being of the Body.

It is frequently pointed out that the Greek term for the gift of knowledge is two words, sometimes translated "word of knowledge." It could also be translated "the ability to speak with knowledge." Those who have this gift are superior learners. They are expected to be among the first to discover new truth and to originate new ideas. They are eager to learn, they have a long attention span, and they are able to absorb and retain unusual amounts of information. Many of them are scholars, at home with research, and are often found in the academic world. Unless they have other gifts in their gift-mix that would counteract this, those who have the gift of knowledge usually have a relatively low need for people. They are more comfortable with ideas than with people. Gossiping is usually not one of their temptations—in fact, it bores them terribly.

I will mention this point later, but I feel that it is needed here as well. In charismatic and Pentecostal circles, it is common to hear "word of knowledge" used in a different sense. It refers to an immediate revelation from God that the person or the church needs to know at the moment. Some people who have a healing ministry might receive a word of knowledge that God wants to heal hernias tonight, that a person suffering a hearing loss in the left ear will be healed or that God wants us to cast out the spirit of nicotine, just to suggest a few examples. In my opinion, this phenomenon, which certainly has proven to be authentic, should be included under the gift of prophecy, not under the gift of knowledge.

KNOWLEDGE GIFT-MIXES

Sometimes the gift of knowledge is associated with others gifts. The gifts of teaching and missionary are two that often are given along with the gift of knowledge.

Knowledge and Teaching

When a person's gift of knowledge is associated with the gift of teaching, I call that person a scholar-teacher. That happens to be one of my strongest gift-mixes. But sometimes the gift of teacher is not added to the gift of knowledge. Some pure scholars have vast amounts of knowledge, have the ability to figure out intricate relationships between ideas and are brilliant at solving intellectual problems, but they have little feeling for the needs of a given audience. In a classroom, they tend to be boring and irrelevant, and few people learn much from them. Such individuals have the gift of knowledge, but not the gift of teacher.

On the other hand, some scholar-teachers might not have the great intellectual capacities that I just described, because much of their energy is, instead, invested in working out ways and means to communicate effectively the knowledge they have accumulated. They have an intuition that tells them what to include in a lecture and what to leave out. They know when to pause, how to use body language, how to vary the voice and how to make use of visuals of one kind or another. They have a sense of timing about when to introduce a new idea or concept. They know how to stimulate and guide discussion. They have a feeling about when discussion is helping the class or when it is becoming irrelevant; then they cut it off at the right moment. This is the gift of teacher.

People who have the gift of knowledge often cannot explain where all their ideas come from. When they need them, the ideas just seem to pop up. But such people need time by themselves for idea development, which may explain why many who have the gift of knowledge seem to be irritated by having too many people around them. Seminary professors frequently joke with one another by saying, "This seminary would be a wonderful place if it just weren't for the students!" That is why, as I have explained, I like to be left alone on a long airplane flight. At 35,000 feet, ideas seem to come to me in unusual quantities.

Knowledge and Missionary

Some of those who have the gift of knowledge and are making a direct contribution to the spread of the gospel are Bible translators. Wycliffe Bible Translators, Lutheran Bible Translators and the several Bible societies around the world recruit translators who have the gift of knowledge, often combined with the gift of missionary. The hours and hours of patient search for words and concepts in an unwritten language require incredible concentration. Because these people have the gift, translators value their agony and isolation, a kind of joy with which few others in the Body can personally identify. Most Christians are glad that someone is translating the Bible in hundreds of remote jungle villages, but they are also glad it is someone else. Together the translators and nontranslators can praise God for spiritual gifts!

THE GIFT OF **WISDOM**

The gift of wisdom is the special ability that God gives to certain members of the Body of Christ to know the mind of the Holy Spirit in such a way as to receive insight into how given knowledge may best be applied to specific needs arising in the Body of Christ.

Those who have the gift of wisdom know how to get to the heart of a problem quickly. They have practical minds and are problem solvers. They have little difficulty in making decisions because they can foresee with a fairly high degree of accuracy what the outcome of the decisions will be. When those with the gift of wisdom speak, other members of the Body recognize that truth has been spoken and the right course of action recommended. Formal learning is not at all a prerequisite. Long hours of digging out new facts may not appeal at all to those who have the gift of wisdom.

One of my good friends who has the gift of wisdom is Leighton Ford. I have already mentioned that he has the gift of evangelist, but he has another gift in his mix. For years, while Leighton Ford was the chair of the Lausanne Committee on World Evangelization, I personally observed him closely, particularly in executive committee meetings, where most of the tough decisions were made. The executive committee was a motley group of high-powered people who had strong opinions on almost every issue imaginable. I frequently found myself in the midst of discussions where the points of view were so divergent that no human way of reconciling them seemed possible.

But Ford had the unusual ability to stay above the give-and-take, not to get involved in the emotions of the discussion, but at just the right time to come up with a suggestion for action that sounded exactly right to the other members of the committee. The gift of wisdom provided him with sensitivity about what each person was trying to say, to what extent he or she was willing to negotiate and what particular personal needs each one had at the moment. His gift was confirmed by a feeling on the part of all members that their point of view had been adequately heard and fairly considered. The result was both individual satisfaction and group harmony.

I personally seem to be at my best developing new hypotheses from information I gather from field research and from observing trends. Then I present my findings in the classroom; I receive feedback from my students, most of whom are leaders in their own right; I revise my original hypotheses; and I later put the results in a book. This, I believe, is the gift of knowledge.

However, when it comes to sitting down with Reverend John Doe who wants to know what he should do in his own parish with all these theories I have fed him, I am in trouble. At this point, I need to rely on someone on my team who understands what I am saying, but who also has the gift of wisdom and who can, consequently, show John Doe how to apply it. Theoreticians like me, who have the gift of knowledge, cannot get the job done without teaming with practitioners, who have the gift of wisdom.

THE GIFTS OF MERCY, HELPS AND SERVICE

It appears to me that the gifts of mercy, helps and service are high-percentage gifts. Although they are found in larger numbers than many other gifts, they also have a fairly low visibility. These are gifts that do not attract much attention or much publicity. Few people become famous for helping others. For every apostle, evangelist or prophet, probably 100 people who have gifts of mercy, helps or service are needed to keep the whole Body healthy. I believe the Bible makes special mention of them in 1 Corinthians 12:22, where it says, "Those members of the body which seem to be weaker are necessary."

THE GIFT OF MERCY

The gift of mercy is the special ability that God gives to certain members of the Body of Christ to feel genuine empathy and compassion for individuals, both Christian and non-Christian, who suffer distressing physical, mental or emotional problems, and to translate that compassion into cheerfully done deeds that reflect Christ's love and alleviate the suffering.

Those who have the gift of mercy engage in one-on-one relationships. They seek out those who need help and develop a personal ministry with them. They show a practical, compassionate love. Their kindness comes naturally and expects no repayment. While the gift of exhortation helps people mainly through *words* of love, the gift of mercy helps people mainly through *deeds* of love.

The recipients of the gift of mercy are the ill, the disabled, the prisoners, the blind, the poor, the aged, the handicapped, the shut-ins, the homeless and the mentally ill. The gift is directed toward both believers and unbelievers. It involves giving a cup of cold water in the name of Jesus.

Every Christian is expected to be merciful. This is a role that reflects the fruit of the Spirit. But those who have the gift of mercy incorporate compassion and kindness into their lifestyle. They do not simply react to emergencies, as every Christian is expected to do. They continually seek opportunities to show pity for those who are down-and-out.

Recently I visited apostle Sunday Adelaja in Kiev, Ukraine. He gave me a personal tour of the Soup Kitchen, which is a ministry of his church, The Embassy of the Blessed Kingdom of God for All Nations. What did I see?

This center cares for no fewer than 1,000 to 2,000 homeless persons per day. When the people come in, they register and leave their ragtag belongings in a safe place. They are taken to an immaculate bath house, where they remove their clothes and shower. They are given other clothes, and the clothes they came with are laundered and returned the same day. During this process they are examined for lice. If they have lice, there is another section into which they must go for complete disinfecting of the individuals as well as of their clothes. Those who require it are then taken to the clinic, where they receive a complete medical examination by doctors, followed by whatever treatment is indicated. When they are bathed, treated and dressed, they are escorted to a gathering place where a resident evangelist explains the gospel to them. Many receive Christ. Then they are taken to the dining room, where they are fed and released. They are allowed to come once a day as long as they need to.

The gift of mercy? I have never before or since seen it operate on such a scale. The huge soup kitchen staff, both paid and volunteer, love what they are doing. They are fulfilled because they are ministering with a spiritual gift that God has chosen to give them. Little wonder that, at the time of this writing, The Embassy of the Blessed Kingdom of God for All Nations, with 25,000 members, is the largest church in Europe.

THE GIFT OF **HELPS**

By sheer coincidence, I drafted this chapter during National Administrative Assistants' Week. Although I am thankful for my gifts, I fully realize that without the help of my administrative assistants, my gifts would instantly drop to less than 50 percent effectiveness. The fruitful exercise of my gifts is highly dependent on the gift of helps.

The gift of helps is the special ability that God gives to certain members of the Body of Christ to invest the talents they have in the life and ministry of other members of the Body, thus enabling those others to increase the effectiveness of their own spiritual gifts.

I once heard Raymond Ortlund describe people who have the gift of helps as the glorious company of the stretcher-bearers. He was referring to the four men who carried their paralyzed friend to Jesus, as recorded in Mark 2:1-12. They remain nameless in Scripture!

Like the gift of mercy, the gift of helps is usually a one-on-

one ministry. Unlike the gift of mercy, however, the recipients of the benefits are not ordinarily the down-and-out, but other Christians exercising their respective gifts.

Two varieties of the gift of helps impress me tremendously. One is editors. I find myself to be a terrible editor. I dislike working on other people's material. When I was teaching in seminary, graduate students who selected me as their mentor knew that they were largely on their own for their theses or dissertations. Many of my faculty colleagues, however, seemed to have the gift of helps and demonstrated it by spending hours on editing and even rewriting for the students. I find that my books are greatly improved between the manuscript stage and the printed page by the editors whom the publishers assign to polish the work. I am ever so grateful to people who have this kind of ministry of helps.

The ultimate example of people who have the gift of helps has to be ghostwriters. Some Christian celebrities produce books that are largely written by other people who never so much as get their name in a byline. It must be because it is so foreign to my own gift-mix that I have developed huge admiration for those to whom God has given the gift of helps in order to do such a wonderful thing for other people.

When spiritual gifts are mobilized in any given local church, a large percentage of people will undoubtedly find that their gift is the gift of helps. And what a relief they will be to pastors and other leaders who are otherwise overworked by a hundred necessary jobs that may have little to do with ministering in their own spiritual gifts.

THE GIFT OF **SERVICE**

Many Bible versions translate the Greek word for the gift of service as "ministry," which is literally correct. But because "ministry" is a rather technical word in our contemporary religious language here in the United States, I think it is less confusing to use "service." In most cases, this gift has little to do with functioning as the professional minister (or senior pastor) of a church. And in a broad sense, every gift—not just this one—is for ministry (see Eph. 4:12).

Actually, the Greek *diakonos* (minister or servant) is also our word for "deacon." In some churches, the job description of deacons requires gifts other than just the gift of service. Originally, however, a deacon was simply one who served others.

The gift of service—sometimes called the gift of volunteer—is the special ability that God gives to certain members of the Body of Christ to identify the unmet needs involved in a task related to God's work, and to make use of available resources to meet those needs and help accomplish the desired goals.

The gift of service is not a one-on-one, person-centered gift as are the gifts of mercy and helps. It is more task oriented. The service is usually directed to an institution and its goals rather than to a particular person. People who have this gift often have a wide range of abilities and talents that they can offer when needs arise. They can be counted on for almost any kind of help. It is another quiet gift, one that does not usually make headlines. Some have suggested that it be called the gift of volunteer.

THE GIFTS OF PROPHECY, TONGUES AND INTERPRETATION OF TONGUES

The three gifts of prophecy, tongues and interpretation of tongues fall naturally together in a cluster because they, more than other gifts (except possibly the gifts of faith and discernment of spirits), are what might be called revelatory gifts. By this I mean that new information from God is transmitted directly to human beings through the person with the gift. Revelation of a kind actually occurs. This is not to be confused with the revelation of God contained in Scripture. I believe that Scripture is inerrant in all it affirms and that God did a special thing in inspiring the authors of Scripture to preserve the unique place of the Bible among all of the world's writings. The Bible is the written Word of God, and none other exists.

> ## The gifts of prophecy, tongues and interpretation of tongues do not transmit *the* Word *of* God; rather they transmit *a* word *from* God.

The three gifts we are discussing here do not transmit *the* Word *of* God; rather they transmit *a* word *from* God. The people who convey God's word through spiritual gifts are not inerrant. Revelation that comes through prophecy or tongues is always subject to examination in light of the written Word of God. The first test of whether a prophecy is true has to be its conformity to the Scriptures. For example, I vaguely recall that years ago a man drove his car at 80 miles an hour through the busy streets of an Ohio city and killed three people. When interviewed later, he said he did it because God told him to. We know this was a false prophecy because it cannot be reconciled with the ethical teachings of the Bible or the nature of the true God.

Those Christians who have the gift of discernment of spirits are usually able to tell the difference between true prophecy and false prophecy. They should be encouraged in the exercise of that gift. For the rest of us, distinguishing between true and false prophecy may be more difficult, but certainly not impossible.

A mistake that enthusiastic believers sometimes make when they discover they have the gifts of prophecy and/or tongues is to pull back on studying, teaching and preaching the Bible. They wrongly feel that these gifts, which are more direct and require less effort than lengthy Bible study, are all they need. The gifts might be true gifts, but the believers who see them in this light misuse them. Anything that dilutes the supreme and unquestioned authority of the Scriptures must be resisted as a ploy of the devil.

At the other extreme are the people who try to deny that God speaks today through prophecy and tongues because these people are so fervent in their desire to preserve the uniqueness and authority of Scripture. Their motive is commendable, but they need to understand that this is not an either-or decision; it is both-and. The combination of biblical teaching about the gifts and the experience of innumerable mature Christian brothers and sisters forces us to the conclusion that God does speak today in a direct and specific way to particular needs and situations just as He did among the ancient people of Israel and among Christians in the first century. His chief (but not exclusive) vehicles for doing this are the gifts of prophecy, tongues and interpretation of tongues.

THE GIFT OF PROPHECY

The gift of prophecy is the special ability that God gives to certain members of the Body of Christ to receive and communicate an immediate message of God to His people through a divinely anointed utterance.

Because the word "prophecy" today usually refers to predicting the future, some people find it difficult to realize that the biblical use of the word includes not only the future but also the present. The gift of prophecy has been used much more for dealing with present situations than with future events. The meaning of the Greek word for "prophecy" is basically "to speak forth" or "to speak for another." Those who have the gift of prophecy receive personal inspiration about God's purpose in concrete situations. God speaks through prophets.

Prophets can err. Therefore they must be open to correction by the rest of the Body. True prophets are willing to be corrected. They want their words to be tested; and when they are wrong, they will openly admit it. They want their prophecies to be confirmed by the Word of God and by the Body as a whole.

Those who receive the benefit of the gift of prophecy can expect comfort, guidance, warning, encouragement, admonition, judgment and edification. God directs some prophecies to individuals and some to the Body of Christ as a whole. In any case, the prophecies should be received as authentic and authoritative messages. As British author Michael Green says, "The Spirit has taken over and addresses the hearers directly through [the prophet]. That is the essence of prophecy."[2] Once the spiritual gift is confirmed by the Body, the person who has the gift should be highly respected, and his or her words should be received with confidence.

In recent times, given the advent of the Second Apostolic Age, prophets have begun to gain a higher visibility in the

Church than previously. This has come about largely through a more literal interpretation of Scriptures such as Ephesians 2:20, which affirms that the foundation of the Church is apostles and prophets with Jesus as the chief cornerstone, as well as 1 Corinthians 12:28, which states, "God has appointed these in the church: first apostles, second prophets." For example, for years, my gift of apostle has been reinforced by Chuck Pierce's gift of prophet, and together we are both more effective in ministry than we could be otherwise.

PROPHECY AND KNOWLEDGE

Previously I mentioned the disagreement I have with some authors in Pentecostal and charismatic traditions concerning the relationship between the gift of knowledge and the gift of prophecy. Let me expand on it a bit more. These authors would not agree with the definition of the gift of knowledge I proposed earlier in this chapter. They tend to define the gift of the "word of knowledge" in much the same way that I have defined the gift of prophecy. I have studied this point of view fairly carefully. One thing I have noticed is that such authors have a difficult time clearly distinguishing between the gift of knowledge, the gift of wisdom and the gift of prophecy. The three appear to be almost synonymous in their writings.[3]

Respected theologian Wayne Grudem agrees. In his article "Wisdom and Knowledge," he affirms his belief that God gives specific revelations to people from time to time. Then he asks, "What *label* should we put on the reporting of these revelations? Should we call them 'words of wisdom' or 'words of knowledge' from time to time, even though the New Testament gives us no justification for attaching such a label?" His answer is no, because the word "prophecy" is the technical New Testament term used to describe such phenomena.[4]

A fine book on words of knowledge, *Hear His Voice*, has been written by Douglas Wead. As I read the book, I began to conclude that he was really writing on the gift of prophecy under another name. I was therefore gratified when I came to a passage where Wead admits, "Some will maintain that [the word of knowledge] should be categorized as a part of the gift of prophecy."[5] I for one do, but I also agree with Wead's statement in which he affirms that no matter what name we give it, "this ability to receive information through extrasensory means was a gift which operated in the New Testament Church as a gift of the Holy Spirit."[6]

I was relieved to see that not all classical Pentecostals hold this view of the gift of knowledge. Pentecostal biblical scholar Donald Gee, for example, tends to agree with me that the gift of knowledge relates more to teaching than it does to prophecy, and he has a long section in his book *Concerning Spiritual Gifts* in which he argues his point.[7] In doing so, he at the same time says, "I wish especially to make clear that I have welcomed interpretations that differ from my own regarding the word of wisdom and the word of knowledge." So do I, mainly because I believe the label one gives to the phenomenon makes little difference in the long run for the health of the Church. I must admit that when addressing certain groups, I even use "word of knowledge" in the popular rather than the technical sense, simply because at that moment I do not feel I should take the time to explain the subtleties.

WHAT PROPHECY LOOKS LIKE

Some who are not familiar with the gift of prophecy firsthand might be wishing at this point for an example of how it works. Many of the books on spiritual gifts written from the charismatic point of view give numerous examples. I most highly recommend Bill Hamon's *Prophets and Personal Prophecy*.[8] The book by Douglas Wead that I referred to earlier is also packed with illustrations of prophecy (although he attributes them to the word of knowledge). To conclude, let me select one of Wead's anecdotes involving the well-known master of ceremonies on *The 700 Club*, Pat Robertson.

Robertson tells the story about a telecast:

> As we were praying God showed me that there was a person whose right forearm had been broken and was in a cast. God was healing it. As I was leaving the studio at the end of the program, I was approached by two women in their middle years. The older of the two had her forearm in a cast. When I saw her, I was asked to pray for them. I replied, "the work has already been done."[9]

Sure enough. The lady returned to her doctor, who x-rayed the arm and found that the bone, which had been crushed, was mended and had almost two inches of new bone tissue. The arm had been healed, and the physician removed the cast. This is a fairly frequent occurrence for Robertson, who apparently has the gift of prophecy and also uses it.

THE GIFT OF TONGUES

A great deal has been written about the gift of tongues because, by far, it has been the most controversial of all the spiritual gifts. Sparking the controversy is the teaching in some circles that speaking in tongues is the initial physical evidence of having received the baptism in the Holy Spirit. The foreseeable outcome of this is to separate the Body of Christ into first-class Christians and second-class Christians simply on the basis of whether or not they have spoken in tongues. Fortunately, the initial-evidence doctrine is not held as rigidly by many today as it once was.

A foremost spokesperson for the classical Pentecostal wing of the church, Jack Hayford, has written a widely acclaimed book on tongues, *The Beauty of Spiritual Language*. Although in the book Hayford advocates speaking in tongues, he also disclaims the narrow initial-evidence doctrine. Jack Hayford believes that tongues might not be essential for a Spirit-filled life, but, he adds, things will usually go better with tongues than without them! Hayford writes, "As readily as I want to honor my Pentecostal forbearers for preserving the testimony of tongues and for generating a passion for Spirit-fullness among millions, at the same time I confess that I believe an unintended but nonetheless restrictive barrier was built. . . . I am referring to a classical Pentecostal conviction: the historic tradition that requires tongues as the 'evidence,' verifying the validity, of a person's being baptized in the Spirit."[10]

The gift of tongues is the special ability that God gives to certain members of the Body of Christ (1) to speak to God in a language they have never learned and/or (2) to receive and communicate an immediate message from God to His people through a divinely anointed utterance in a language they have never learned.

The gift of tongues is the only 1 of the 28 gifts that I think must be broken down into two parts. The first variety of the gift of tongues might be called private tongues and the second variety public tongues.

Private tongues are often referred to as a prayer language. No accompanying gift of interpretation need be involved. The biblical text most descriptive of this is 1 Corinthians 14:28, where

Paul says that tongues without interpretation should not be used in the church, but rather the person who has such a gift should "speak to himself and to God." Because this is highly experiential, I am going to describe it by using the experiences of a Christian brother.

Robert Tuttle is an esteemed United Methodist leader and teacher. One of his gifts is private tongues. He writes, "There are times in my devotional life when I can no longer find words to express my 'innards.' . . . At that point I allow the Holy Spirit to pray through me in a language that I did not learn. Believe me, I know what it means to learn a language. I struggle with the biblical languages every day. . . . I say a language because I believe it to be a language. My vocabulary is growing. I know enough about language to be able to identify sentence structure. My unknown tongue or prayer language has periods, commas, and exclamation points. It is a marvelous gift."[11]

Some people will raise the question as to what good private tongues does. I have been helped a great deal by Harold Bredesen, who lists these five functions:

1. Tongues enables our spirits to communicate directly with God above and beyond the power of our minds to understand.
2. Tongues liberates the Spirit of God within us.
3. Tongues enables the Spirit to take its place of ascendancy over soul and body.
4. Tongues is God's provision for catharsis, therefore important to our mental health.
5. Tongues meets our needs for a whole new language for worship, prayer and praise.[12]

These statements need little comment. Without question,

they reflect the self-perception of one who has and uses the gift of private tongues, and I think that others would agree on their validity.

PROJECTING TONGUES

I suppose that the gift of private tongues is the most frequently projected of all the spiritual gifts. People who have it find it so simple and so natural that they are inclined to conclude that anybody can do it. They may quote Paul's statement, "I wish you all spoke with tongues" (1 Cor. 14:5), but perhaps they make it mean more than Paul intended in the context of the abuse of tongues in Corinth.

If there is any such thing as a *role* of tongues, I suppose it would fit here, but perhaps this is one gift that has no universal corresponding role. Those Pentecostals and charismatics who do not agree with Jack Hayford expect all Christians to speak in tongues at least once, thereby proving that they are baptized in the Holy Spirit. To these Pentecostals and charismatics, it would be a Christian role. In my view, our common Christian role is being open for the Holy Spirit to allow us to speak in tongues if and when He wishes. Meanwhile, I know that some wonderfully mature Christian brothers and sisters have sincerely desired to pray in tongues but with no success. To say that they have not been filled with the Spirit would, in many cases, be both inaccurate and pastorally insensitive. My wife, Doris, is a case in point. She is more than open to speak in tongues, but at least at this writing she has never done so. Yet she is one whom people seek out from near and far to cast out demons. She has the spiritual gift of deliverance but not the spiritual gift of tongues, much to the puzzlement of some Pentecostal brothers and sisters.

THE GIFT OF
INTERPRETATION OF TONGUES

The second variety of the gift of tongues, public tongues, is inti-
mately related to the gift of interpretation of tongues. Without
interpretation, the gift of tongues is useless and has no part in
the Church (see 1 Cor. 14:27-28).

*The gift of interpretation of tongues is the special ability that God
gives to certain members of the Body of Christ to make known in
the vernacular the message of one who speaks in tongues.*

Often, but not always, tongues-interpretation functions as a
hyphenated gift. Michael Green says, "Though some have the
gift of interpretation who cannot themselves speak in tongues,
this is unusual; for the most part it is those who already have
tongues who gain this further gift of interpretation."[13] Some
people give messages in public in tongues and immediately
interpret what they themselves have said. In other cases, one person will give the message and another one will interpret.

A question is frequently raised whether interpretation of
tongues is the equivalent of translation. In most cases, if not
all, the answer is no. The person who has the gift of interpretation is normally given the sense of the message by the Holy
Spirit, not a linguistic understanding of the grammar and
vocabulary. At the same time, frequent reports have come of
the message in tongues being perfectly understood by someone
present who has recognized it as their mother tongue, a literal
foreign language.

Not much more needs to be said about public tongues
except that it is a functional equivalent to prophecy. The whole
argument of 1 Corinthians 14 develops this equivalence. What
we previously said about the gift of prophecy, then, applies

equally to public tongues with interpretation.

As an example, I will relate a secondhand anecdote I received from a reliable source. It involves a group of believers in a remote Guatemalan village. A severe drought had devastated the area, and the village was on the verge of extinction. The Christians prayed, and God spoke to the group through a message in tongues with interpretation. God told them to go up on a hill, which was owned by Christians, and to dig a well. It seemed to be one of the most illogical places to dig a well, but they obeyed, facing the potential ridicule of the unbelievers in the village. The ridicule changed to astonishment, however, when they soon struck an abundant supply of water, and the entire village was saved from extinction. Many unbelievers also were saved spiritually when they saw the power of God. Perhaps this is what Paul had in mind when he wrote, "Tongues are for a sign, not to those who believe but to unbelievers" (1 Cor. 14:22).

One rather parenthetical observation needs to be made before moving on to another cluster of gifts. Some people have gone as missionaries to other linguistic groups and have begun speaking the second language without ever having learned it. Documentation of this is abundant enough to satisfy me. Is this the gift of tongues? In my opinion, no. Rather, I regard it as a miracle that God chose to perform on that certain occasion. I am encouraged to find that one of the key classical Pentecostal authors, Donald Gee, agrees with me concerning this point.[14]

THE GIFTS OF MIRACLES AND HEALING

Whereas prophecy and tongues are immediate *words* of supernatural origin, miracles and healing are immediate *deeds* of supernatural origin. In both cases, human beings who have spiritual gifts are the instruments through which God does a remarkable work.

THE GIFT OF MIRACLES

The gift of miracles is the special ability that God gives to certain members of the Body of Christ to serve as human intermediaries through whom it pleases God to perform powerful acts that are perceived by observers to have altered the ordinary course of nature.

Notice that this definition does not close the door to the performance of miracles that may later be "disproved" by the application of Western scientific methods. For example, I have read lengthy attempts to explain why people who were raised from the dead in Indonesia were not really raised from the dead. Apparently, some Western investigators went to Indonesia and concluded that—according to their Western definitions of death—no one was raised from the dead. The individuals were only awakened from comas.

This would be amusing if it were not so pathetic. God performed the miracles for Indonesians, not for Americans or Europeans. If Indonesians, both believers and unbelievers, really and truly thought that the dead had been raised, then the miracle happened. Indonesians know as well as Americans when a person dies. What is the purpose of attempting to disprove such a thing? If through observing this, Indonesian believers were strengthened in their faith and Indonesian unbelievers were convinced of the power of God and became followers of Jesus Christ, the purpose of the miracle was accomplished.

Because of our innate commitment to naturalism, we

Westerners tend to be suspect of anything clearly supernatural. That is undoubtedly one reason why we do not see as many miracles working in our churches here today as we seem to hear about from the mission field. But this does not justify looking with sophisticated skepticism on the working of God's miracles in other cultures that are much more open to supernaturalism than our own.

And my perception is that our own culture is gradually becoming more open to supernaturalism. The increasing popularity of the transcendent; the rise of Eastern religions, the New Age and the occult; along with the phenomenal expansion of the charismatic movement itself—all are indicators that many Americans may be fed up with the unsatisfying secular humanism that modern science and technology have attempted to make part and parcel of our culture. If so, the way may be open as never before for the gift of miracles to become more evident in our churches in the United States.

Some people will fear such a manifestation of God's power because the gift so easily can be abused. This is true, but it is not an adequate reason for hastily rejecting the spiritual gift of miracles, it seems to me. Yes, God will and does bless churches that do not encourage miracles. But to justify an aversion to miracles from a *biblical* point of view is not easy. The aversion is probably much more cultural than biblical. I agree with Kenneth Gangel when he says, "We dare not be guided in our understanding of spiritual gifts by a fear born of unhappy experiences nor an exegesis which results from hermeneutical myopia."[15]

THE GIFT OF HEALING

The gift of healing is the special ability that God gives to certain

*members of the Body of Christ to serve as human intermediaries
through whom it pleases God to cure illness and restore health
apart from the use of natural means.*

In one sense, the gift of healing can be understood as a specialized manifestation of the gift of miracles, but the two are mentioned separately in the Bible, so I also like to separate them. Obviously, healing has to do with human illness specifically, although it includes all kinds of human illnesses. The biblical reference to the gift of healing in 1 Corinthians 12:28 is literally "gifts [plural] of healings [plural]." This seems to imply many varieties of the gift for various kinds of illnesses.

To restrict the gift of healing to physical diseases is not proper. The gift can also be used to cure mental, emotional and spiritual illnesses. Agnes Sanford, pioneer of the current restoration of the gift of healing, had a ministry of healing the memory. My colleague, Charles Kraft, is extensively used in inner healing, or, as he prefers to call it, deep-level healing. Some people might argue that the gift of deliverance, or spiritual healing, should be included here instead of being identified as a separate gift. And even other varieties of healing may exist.

The gift of healing does not give a person supernatural power over disease. He or she is simply an instrument through whom God works when He desires to heal. People who have the gift of healing have no power to empty hospitals unless God decides to do that through them. No one fully understands God's position on sickness and health. Sometimes, as we know from Job, sickness is part of the total plan of God, and He permits it. The apostle Paul had a "thorn in the flesh" (2 Cor. 12:7), which in all probability was a physical problem of some kind, but God chose not to remove it. And, furthermore, healing is not permanent. As far as we know, all the people whom Jesus Himself healed eventually died!

The gift of healing does not make doctors and nurses obsolete. In many cases, God is pleased to use modern medical means of healing, although this should not be confused with the gift of healing. Christian doctors by and large are using natural talents, not a spiritual gift. Part of the definition of the gift is "apart from the use of natural means." When Timothy had a stomach ailment, Paul did not send him a handkerchief he had touched so that Timothy could be healed through it. Paul had used the handkerchiefs in Ephesus to good effect (see Acts 19:12), but he recommended wine to Timothy in this case (see 1 Tim. 5:23). Sometimes natural means are in order; sometimes God chooses to heal miraculously. The person with the gift cannot manipulate God. He or she is simply a frequently used instrument.

E. STANLEY JONES'S PRAYERS

God has healed me personally in both spiritual and medical ways. Most of my sicknesses have been cured by doctors or known remedies. One time, however, God cured me directly. Some years ago in Bolivia, I had an open sore on my neck that had been operated on and would not heal, so I was scheduled for further surgery. Then missionary and evangelist E. Stanley Jones came to town and some of us missionaries went to hear him. His meeting turned out to be a healing service. During the service, I knew I had been healed. When I got home, I took off the bandage and saw that the sore was still full of pus. But I thanked the Lord and went to bed; the next morning I was perfectly well. The doctor was astounded, but he was a Christian, so we praised the Lord together! The problem has never returned.

As I have researched the Pentecostal movement in Latin America and analyzed its amazing growth over the past decades, I have found that one of the key factors contributing to its growth is faith healing. Latin American Pentecostals tend to believe that God can and will heal apart from natural means, and He does it frequently in their midst. Non-Pentecostals tend to believe that God *can* heal but not that He *will*, so He does not seem to do it very much at all.[16] If the faith is not there, the healing does not happen, as Jesus' disciples learned. They were "of little faith" (Matt. 8:26), as are so many of us today.

REFLECTIONS

1. Many people do not recognize the differences between the gift of knowledge and the gift of wisdom. Can you clarify the differences?
2. The same is true with the differences between the gift of helps and the gift of service. You probably know people with each of these gifts. Can you name these people?
3. Consider the way many people use the expression "word of knowledge" as if it were the same as the gift of prophecy. Why would Peter Wagner say he sometimes uses "word of knowledge" in a way that he does not agree with in theory?
4. Some churches allow the private exercise of the gift of tongues, but they prohibit public tongues. Do you think this position can be justified?
5. Have you seen miracles and healings in your church? If not, do you think that these gifts might actually be there but have not yet been discovered?

Notes

1. Ralph W. Neighbour, Jr., *This Gift Is Mine* (Nashville, TN: Broadman Press, 1974), p. 72.
2. Michael Green, *I Believe in the Holy Spirit* (Grand Rapids, MI: Eerdmans Publishing Company, 1975), p. 172.
3. See, for example, Harold Horton, *The Gifts of the Spirit* (Springfield, MO: Gospel Publishing Company, 1975), chapters 4 and 5; and Jim McNair, *Love and Gifts* (Minneapolis, MN: Bethany Fellowship, 1976), p. 26.
4. Wayne Grudem, "Wisdom and Knowledge," *Ministries Today* (January/February 1993), p. 64.
5. R. Douglas Wead, *Hear His Voice* (Carol Stream, IL: Creation House, 1976), p. 100.
6. Ibid.
7. Donald Gee, *Concerning Spiritual Gifts* (Springfield, MO: Gospel Publishing House, 1972), pp. 111-119.
8. Bill Hamon, *Prophets and Personal Prophecy* (Point Washington, FL: Christian International Publishers, 1987).
9. Pat Robertson, quoted in Wead, *Hear His Voice*, p. 120.
10. Jack Hayford, *The Beauty of Spiritual Language* (Dallas: Word Books, 1992), p. 92.
11. Robert G. Tuttle, *The Partakers* (Nashville, TN: Abingdon Press, 1974), p. 82.
12. Harold Bredesen, "The Gift of Tongues," *Logos Journal* (March 1978), pp. 19-24.
13. Green, *I Believe in the Holy Spirit*, p. 167.
14. Gee, *Concerning Spiritual Gifts*, p. 97.
15. Kenneth O. Gangel, *You and Your Spiritual Gift* (Chicago: Moody Press, 1975), p. 59.
16. This is expanded in C. Peter Wagner, *Spiritual Power and Church Growth* (Altamonte, FL: Creation House, 1986), chapter 9.

Chapter 10

FIVE STEPS YOUR
CHURCH CAN TAKE TO
GROW THROUGH GIFTS

All the good theories in the world about spiritual gifts will not be worth more than a pleasant head trip if their dynamics are not released for effective operation in local congregations. The purpose of this final chapter is to propose some guidelines on how this can happen.

HINDRANCES TO
THE USE OF SPIRITUAL GIFTS

After only a short time of conversation, it is fairly easy to know whether a given person comes from a church that is aware of spiritual gifts and is encouraging their use. Many Christians are either ignorant or they are surprisingly reluctant about making reference to their own spiritual gifts. Some are unsure. Some feel they would be boasting if they mentioned their gifts. Some do not want to be held accountable for the gifts' use, so they keep them to themselves.

I once was in a meeting of a small group of Christian leaders from around the world. Most of them were considered part of the spiritual elite of their country, and their names would be recognized as Christian household words. In a session of sharing (which I did not lead, incidentally), each one around the circle was asked to praise God for a specific spiritual gift. I quickly took out a pencil to jot down the responses:

"Preach the gospel"
"The Holy Spirit"
"Jesus Christ"
"The life-giving Spirit"
"Billy Graham"
"Loved ones and children"
"Teaching"
"Brothers and sisters in Christ"

I will admit that I was the one who mentioned teaching as the spiritual gift for which I was thankful. I surmise that "preaching the gospel" was meant to refer to the gift of evangelist. But I was disappointed that in this kind of high-visibility group, only 25 percent accurately articulated a biblical spiritual gift. If this had occurred a generation ago, I might have understood it. But since these were leaders, what must the percentage among grassroots Christians have been? As it was in Corinth, considerable ignorance of spiritual gifts is evident (see 1 Cor. 12:1).

This ignorance seems to be on the increase in the United States. As I mentioned in chapter 2, when George Barna did a study of Christians and their spiritual gifts over a five-year period, he was alarmed by the results. In 1995 he found that among born-again adults, 4 percent did not believe that they had a spiritual gift (a reasonable number, in my opinion). However, the same survey in 2000 showed that the 4 percent had risen to 21 percent![1]

Think of what a trend like this might mean. If fewer and fewer believers think they have a spiritual gift, fewer and fewer will be ministering in the Body of Christ in the way that God has designed them to minister. The predictable outcome will be weaker and weaker churches.

PASTORS, THE TIME IS NOW

My word to Christian leaders is to act now and to help your people move in spiritual gifts before it is too late. The time is ripe for Christians all over the world, in every church, to begin to think soberly of themselves (see Rom. 12:3). They must not do this, of course, by adopting any air of pride. But neither should they do it by putting up a facade of false humility, which blinds them and others around them to the function God has given them in the Body of Christ through their spiritual gifts.

I will outline five steps designed to help get you and your congregation put into operation the wonderful power that God has already provided in the gifts He has given. The five steps are addressed to both clergy and laity, if I may revert to this somewhat antiquated terminology. But I need to stress two assumptions that I am making preliminary to the five steps. I am assuming, first of all, that the pastor of your church is convinced that discovering, developing and using spiritual gifts is the will of God for the congregation, and that he or she is willing to take an active leadership role in the process. Second, I am also assuming that your pastor wants your church to grow and is willing to pay the price.

The two assumptions are based on everything I have tried to say in chapter 6, the chapter on the pastor. The pastor is God's key person for the growth of a local church; and if for some reason or another, he or she is either indifferent or opposed to church growth or spiritual gifts, my advice is to postpone these five steps because, frankly, they can easily backfire. I honestly hope that this book itself will help change the mind of many a reluctant pastor; but if it or other books, seminars or personal exhortations do not do the trick, my advice is to continue to pray and then wait for God's better timing.

STEP 1: AGREE ON A PHILOSOPHY OF MINISTRY

The benefits of each local church having a well-articulated philosophy of ministry have already been mentioned several times. Part of a church's philosophy of ministry ought to be a clear statement on what the church believes and expects in the way of spiritual gifts. If your church has had a stated philosophy of ministry and it does not include a section on spiritual gifts, I suggest that it be amended.

Any program you launch for discovering and using spiritual gifts will be molded by your philosophy of ministry. You need to secure consensus on such things as these:

- Which spiritual gifts do we expect God to give to our church in our particular gift-mix? Are we open to all 28? If not, how many might there be? Will we look for 19 or 9, or how many?
- Are we open to the sign gifts, such as tongues and prophecy and healings? If yes, should they be used in public or only in private? If in public, should they be used in all services or only in certain designated ones?
- Do we believe that baptism in the Holy Spirit is a second work of grace, or do all Christians receive it when they are saved? If a second work of grace, do we believe that speaking in tongues is the initial physical evidence that tells us that it has truly happened to any given individual?

- What positions do we take in regard to new people who come into our church but who disagree with our views on spiritual gifts? Or with current members who change their views? Are we cordial to this, do we just tolerate it or do we recommend that such persons seek fellowship in a more compatible church?

My recommendation is that as the leaders of the church sit down to discuss these issues, they should not become overly self-conscious. Above all, do not make a decision just because so-and-so church down the street does it that way. Consider it with the same spirit with which most of us who are Christians have learned to accept baptism. Some churches baptize infants by sprinkling. Some churches will neither baptize infants nor baptize by sprinkling. Some churches will immerse. Some immersionists dip the person three times instead of only once. Some dip them three times forward and some dip them three times backward. Quakers do not believe in water baptism at all. Some churches do not think that any of the above is essential, so they baptize both infants and adults by either sprinkling or immersion; and I suppose that if people were to request it, they would be willing to baptize them three times forward. If some do not want to be baptized at all, these churches also would accept them and love them on the same basis as the others.

Churches across the United States tend to accept the fact that God leads different churches to establish different philosophies of baptism, and few of us tend to feel self-conscious about the position that we hold. Why not follow this same pattern on spiritual gifts? Let's each decide on our own philosophy of spiritual gifts; let's discover what particular gift-mix God has given each of our churches; and let's praise God for other churches that may have different philosophies of ministry.

I see two immediate benefits in forming a philosophy of ministry. First, Christian unity will be enhanced. It is a tragedy that some local churches have split over spiritual gifts. The chances of this happening are almost nil when a clear philosophy of ministry has been agreed upon. Not only will brothers and sisters in a local church tend to love one another more, but feelings of envy, jealousy, competition or witch-hunting between churches will be greatly reduced. Why not accept each other's differences and love each other in the Lord? I like the title of a book by Peter Gillquist: *Let's Quit Fighting About the Holy Spirit*.[2]

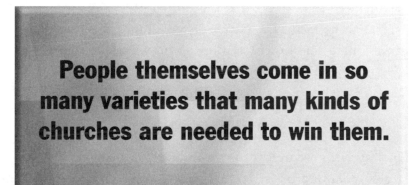

People themselves come in so many varieties that many kinds of churches are needed to win them.

The second benefit can be church growth. The more churches and philosophies of ministry available in the community, the more unbelievers will presumably be won to Christ. People themselves come in so many varieties that many kinds of churches are needed to win them. I think that it would be a setback to effective evangelism if all churches in the city somehow were to become the same. This is why, in most cases, church mergers ultimately end up with fewer members than the separate churches counted before they merged.

STEP 2: INITIATE A GROWTH PROCESS

Discovering, developing and using spiritual gifts can be an end in itself, and it is a good end. In some cases, this alone will help a church grow. But church growth is complex, and the dynamic of spiritual gifts is only one of many church-growth principles. Therefore, in most cases a program of putting spiritual gifts to use will not be sufficient by itself for maximizing the growth potential of a church. When gifts are discovered, they must have channels through which they can be used effectively.

Few things will prove to be more frustrating than discovering a spiritual gift and not being able to use it in the church. Pastors need to be aware that the church will risk losing members if this happens. The members may simply transfer to some other church where they feel more useful.

STEP 3: STRUCTURE FOR GIFTS AND GROWTH

One form of government that is popular in America but that is largely counterproductive for growth, especially in a large church, is a congregational form of government. Most pastors of large, growing churches that have traditionally congregational governments have somehow developed ways and means to streamline the structure. This type of church government may be feasible for smaller churches, but when the membership begins to pass the 200 mark, it becomes less and less effective.

The smoothest structure for growth is one that fully recognizes the leadership position of the pastor, thus freeing the pastor to utilize his or her spiritual gift. In many growing churches, a board runs the church, and the pastor serves as the chairperson of the board and the president of the corporation. When the church has a well-thought-out philosophy of ministry, this can operate well. The more boards and committees in a church, however, the more chances for bickering, infighting and conflict of interests. They slow down the decision-making process, sometimes almost to a standstill.

As I understand God's way of operating, one person, under God, bears the chief responsibility for a local church—that person is the senior pastor. God will hold all members responsible for their church, of course, but none to the degree of the person who has accepted the top position of leadership. I believe that the attitude church members need to have toward their pastor is described in Hebrews 13:17: "Obey your leaders and follow their orders. They watch over your souls without resting, since they must give to God an account of their service. If you obey them, they will do their work gladly; if not, they will do it with sadness, and that would be of no help to you" (*TEV*).

Not enough sermons are preached on the text of Hebrews 13:17. It is extremely difficult for pastors to preach sermons on it in their own churches because their motives could easily be misinterpreted. That is why I continually comment upon and stress it. Because I am not a pastor myself, I have few worries about being misinterpreted. But I do have a pastor over me and I try to apply it in my own attitude toward him and toward the staff. Many pastors are suffering untold personal grief and frustration because their people do not understand or practice the biblical principle of obedience to those in authority. The total effect of overlooking or neglecting this principle is that it becomes an obstruction to church growth.

Another obstacle to church growth is the effect of Parkinson's Law, which says that work increases to fill the time available for doing it. Research done by Kent Tucker indicates that in many churches, 85 percent of available time is given to management and only 15 percent of time is given to ministry.[3] The basic growth problem here is the proportion of available time spent in administrative and organizational matters as compared to the time spent in actual ministry. This is horribly inefficient. No corporation could last a month by having such a structure. Committees and boards can be incredibly busy, but in the end, they may get very little done in terms of the ministry objectives of the church.

To illustrate this issue, Kent Tucker reported what occurred at the First Baptist Church of Modesto, California. When Pastor Bill Yaeger arrived, he discovered Parkinson's Law at work. So he streamlined the church administration, and the church began to grow faster as a result. Previously, the church had showed a decadal decline of 0.8 percent. Over a period of 10 years, only three new converts had been baptized. Under Yaeger's leadership, however, the church reorganized its structure by going from a multiple-board church to a one-board church. Yaeger said, "When we have this simplified organizational structure, people are then free to be involved in evangelism and discipleship."[4] After restructuring, they calculated that 97.1 percent of the time that laypeople volunteered to the church went into ministry, and only 2.9 percent went toward managing the affairs of the church. The decadal growth rate of First Baptist over the 10 years following the change soared to 388 percent. The church staunchly refused to allow Parkinson's Law to halt its growth.

Once people are freed from organizational duties for which most are not gifted, they can then use their spiritual gifts in ministries for which they are more suited. After carefully studying their church's structure, many church leaders are surprised to find out how inefficiently their church members are deployed.

STEP 4: UNWRAP
THE SPIRITUAL GIFTS

Think of your church experience as Christmas Day. The tree is set up and decorated, and the gifts are placed underneath and waiting for the family to unwrap them. Your church is ready to grow. God has provided the gifts, but few people know what they are. Now is the time to unwrap them!

As I see it, a checklist of five items should be considered for processing and developing a strong dynamic of spiritual gifts in your church.

1. Motivate the Congregation
from the Pulpit

Because pastors need to lead their churches into growth, their ideas need to be heard from the pulpit. One pastor I know of preached 22 consecutive sermons on spiritual gifts and had dramatic results, both in terms of people finding their own gifts and in explosive church growth. Many other pastors have testified that a series of sermons on spiritual gifts has made a visible difference in church growth. Pastors of churches that become structured around spiritual gifts not only preach such series but also continually mention spiritual gifts in their other sermons. And they do not assume one series of sermons is enough. Year after year they preach on the subject from different points of view to inform new members and to reinforce older members.

When the pastor teaches a lot about spiritual gifts, it makes it easier for the people to talk about them with each other. They realize that it is the in thing, and the tone created by a strong pulpit ministry on gifts can be helpful in all areas of church life.

2. Study the Biblical Teaching on Gifts

Not only should the people hear about spiritual gifts from the pulpit, but they themselves should also study the gifts. This can be done in small groups, in special study sessions, in Sunday School classes or at home in private.

In order to facilitate this, I have developed a user-friendly study guide based on this book. It is a convenient manual of 12 lessons, each one with full do-it-yourself instructions for the teacher for either a 60-minute session or a 90-minute session. Purchasing the study guide authorizes you to reproduce it for your church or Sunday School class or home group or whomever you teach, including the Wagner-Modified Houts Questionnaire, which each person in the group can fill out and score. It is published by Regal, so your local Christian bookstore can get it for you. The name? *Your Spiritual Gifts Can Help Your Church Grow Small Group Study Guide.*

A Bible study like this will help the whole congregation become familiar with what the gifts are, how the gifts fit together to form the Body of Christ and what the gifts might mean to each person individually.

3. Help Adults Discover Their Gifts

I have used the word "adults" advisedly here, because not every Christian of every age is ready for coming to terms with his or her spiritual gift. My rule of thumb is that if you are 18 years old and do not know your spiritual gift, do not worry; you are probably too young. If you are 25, however, and still do not know your spiritual gift, it is time to start worrying. The ability to discover spiritual gifts, in my understanding, is a function of emotional maturity. Emotionally mature people are ready to know their gifts, but emotional maturity comes at different ages for different people. Some are emotionally mature at 20; others are not yet emotionally mature at 30.

New Christians who are emotionally mature should be expected to discover their gifts within 4 to 12 months after accepting Christ as Lord and Savior, depending on a variety of factors. One of the first things that all new believers should learn is that God has given them at least one spiritual gift, which God is waiting for them to discover.

4. Set a Schedule for Accountability

Some churches make the mistake of holding a spiritual gifts workshop as if it were just another pleasant and inspiring program event. When it is over, the churches go on to begin some other interesting project. Unfortunately, no definite plans are made to follow through, so the net result in some cases is negligible as far as church growth is concerned.

As the spiritual gifts process gets under way in your church, be sure to set goals for the discovery of spiritual gifts. Two good goals for your church might be that 50 percent of the adults will be able to describe their own spiritual gift in 12 months and that 20 percent more adults will be in the process of discovery. Each group needs to develop some system to see that it happens. People need to be held accountable to each other for discovering their gifts and then for using them. I promise you that this will be an enjoyable experience for all.

5. Continue the Experience Indefinitely

Discovering, developing and using spiritual gifts should be no more an on-again, off-again part of church life than, say, prayer or Bible study or Communion. The experience should become a permanent part of the lifestyle of the congregation. It needs to be stimulated with books, sermons, Sunday School lessons and task-oriented groups that help people put their gifts to use. Timothy apparently let his gift of evangelist fall into disuse and Paul had to prod him (see 1 Tim. 4:14). It will happen to us also if we are not on guard.

Perhaps the action of St. Paul Lutheran Church in Detroit, Michigan, could be an example to others who are interested in building spiritual gifts into their growth process. The church, which showed a healthy growth rate, found spiritual gifts to be a vital key. As a result, Pastor Wayne Pohl added a new full-time staff member, Arthur Beyer, who held the title "minister of spiritual gifts," in order to help maintain the growth.

STEP 5: EXPECT GOD'S BLESSING

Teaching on spiritual gifts was not invented by some management-efficiency consultant or by some department of church growth or by some theological seminary or by some church council. The teaching on spiritual gifts comes directly from the Word of God. This gives us the assurance we need to say with confidence that it is truly God's way for His people to operate with one another. It is the way to do God's work, whether caring for each other or learning more about the faith or celebrating the resurrection of Jesus Christ or reaching out to the lost with the message of God's love. It is the way to bring about the kind of healthy church growth that builds the whole person and the whole Body of Christ.

Faith is the key. Without faith it is impossible to please God (see Heb. 11:6). Faith is expectation—expectation that God has something better for us, expectation that we can be the people God wants us to be, expectation that He has gifted us and expectation that we will be richly fulfilled if we are doing His will through using our spiritual gifts.

Faith tells us that God wants His Church to grow. He wants His lost sheep found and brought into the fold. And He desires to do it through the gifts He has given to each of us for His glory.

REFLECTIONS

1. As has been said frequently, the leadership role of the pastor is crucial for the health of the local church. What kind of leadership have you seen your pastor give in the area of spiritual gifts?
2. How would your church handle a new member who feels that he or she should begin to minister in a certain spiritual gift that your church frowns upon?
3. Parkinson's Law causes some churches to overwork their laypeople in committees and administration while underutilizing them in areas for which they are really gifted. Rate your church in this regard.
4. How ready is your church to hold one or more spiritual gifts workshops in order to help as many people as possible discover their gifts?
5. Suppose that many people in your church suddenly discovered their spiritual gifts. Do you think your church is ready to put such people to work?

Notes
1. The Barna Group, "Awareness of Spiritual Gifts Is Changing," The Barna Update, February 5, 2001. http://www.barna.org/FlexPage.aspx?Page=BarnaUpdate&BarnaUpdateID=81 (accessed December 10, 2004).
2. Peter E. Gillquist, *Let's Quit Fighting About the Holy Spirit* (Grand Rapids, MI: Zondervan Publishing House, 1974).

3. Kent A. Tucker, "A Church Growth Study of the First Baptist Church of Modesto" (Doctor of Ministry paper, Fuller Seminary, 1978), p. 37.

4. Ibid., p. 38.

WAGNER-MODIFIED HOUTS QUESTIONNAIRE

Greetings!

You are about to become involved in an exciting spiritual exercise. God has given you one or more spiritual gifts if you are a Christian, and discovering that gift or gifts will be a thrilling experience.

You will be asked to consider and score the 135 statements found in the Wagner-Modified Houts Questionnaire. This spiritual gifts discovery instrument has been used throughout the Body of Christ since 1976. The copy you have in your hand is the eighth edition, each one being improved in the light of past experience.

Hundreds of thousands of believers have been blessed by using the Wagner-Modified Houts Questionnaire. You can be confident that it will give you a fairly accurate picture of what kind of ministry God expects you to be carrying out in conjunction with the group of believers with whom you associate.

However, do not regard the results of this test as final. The three or four gifts you score highest on may or may not turn out to be your real spiritual gifts. But you can be sure in any case that they are a starting point for prayer and experimentation. You will need other members of the Body of Christ to help you confirm what gifts you have, as well as what gifts you might not have.

As you go through this questionnaire, you may notice that the gift of martyrdom is not included. The reason for this is that, after many attempts, I have not been able to find a feasible way to test for this gift.

My prayer is that this enjoyable experience will raise you to a brand new level of satisfaction in serving the Lord and blessing other members of the Body of Christ!

C. Peter Wagner

BEFORE YOU START

Follow these four steps:

Step 1   Pray and ask God to guide you, and then go through the list of 135 statements in the questionnaire found on pages 249 through 264. Or you may take this questionnaire on the Internet. To do so, you will need to use your personal identification code, which you will find printed on the inside of this book's dust jacket. Then go to the Spiritual Gifts Finder website at www.spiritualgiftsfinder.com; and when prompted, enter your identification code. The online instructions will guide you through the process of completing the questionnaire. (The website will work with most modern computer systems. To connect to the site, you will need at least a 28.8 modem and version 4 or higher of Internet Explorer, Netscape or AOL.)

Whether you take the questionnaire in this book or online, mark to what extent each statement has been true of your life: Much, Some, Little, or Not at All.

Warning! Do not score according to what you think *should* be true or what you hope *might* be true in the future. For the best results, be honest and score only on the basis of your past experience. In most cases, the answer that comes first to your mind will turn out to be the most valid answer. The more you find yourself pondering, the fuzzier your answer might be.

Step 2   When you are finished, score the questionnaire by using the Wagner-Modified Houts Chart on page

265. If you take the online version, the Spiritual Gifts Finder will score the questionnaire for you.

Step 3   After filling in your scores, you will want to refer to pages 267 through 274 to study the gift definitions and Scripture references to help you evaluate your scores. You will also find these definitions online.

Step 4   Complete the exercises on pages 275 through 277 to gain a tentative evaluation of where your gifts may lie and to explore the implications for your ministry in the Body of Christ. If possible, get together with some others who know you and talk about what you have found.

Reproduction of this questionnaire is prohibited.

STEP 1: WAGNER-MODIFIED HOUTS QUESTIONNAIRE

For each statement, mark to what extent it is true of your life:
<u>M</u>uch, <u>S</u>ome, <u>L</u>ittle or <u>N</u>ot at All

M   S   L   N

1. I have a desire to speak direct messages that I receive from God in order to edify, exhort or comfort others.

2. I have enjoyed ministering to a certain group of people over a long period of time, sharing personally in their successes and their failures.

3. People have told me that I have helped them learn biblical truths in a meaningful way.

4. I have applied spiritual truth effectively to critical situations in my own life.

5. Others have told me I have helped them to discern key and important facts of Scripture.

6. I have verbally encouraged and helped the wavering, the troubled or the discouraged.

7. Others in my church have noted that I am able to see through phoniness before it is evident to other people.

M   S   L   N

8. I find I manage money well in order to give liberally to the Lord's work.

9. I have assisted Christian leaders to relieve them for concentrating on their essential job.

10. I have a desire to work with those who have physical or mental problems in order to alleviate their suffering.

11. I feel comfortable relating to people of other cultures, and they seem to accept me.

12. I have led others to a decision for salvation through faith in Christ.

13. My home is always open to people who need a place to stay.

14. When in a group, I am the one to whom others often look to for vision and direction.

15. When I speak, people seem to listen and agree.

16. When a group I am in is lacking organization, I love to step in to fill the gap.

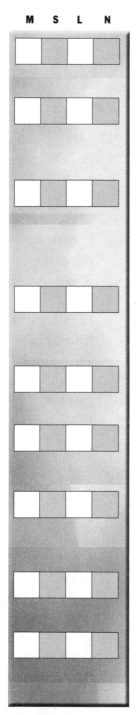

M   S   L   N

17. Others can point to specific in- stances in which my prayers have resulted in visible miracles.

18. In the name of the Lord, I have been used in curing diseases in- stantaneously.

19. I have spoken in tongues.

20. Sometimes when a person speaks in tongues, I seem to know what God is saying through them.

21. I could live more comfortably, but I choose not to in order to identify with the poor.

22. I am single and enjoy it.

23. I spend at least an hour a day in prayer.

24. I have spoken directly to evil spirits, and they have obeyed me.

25. I enjoy being called on to do odd jobs around the church.

26. A number of pastors and/or ministry leaders have told me that they desire to minister and to be held account- able under my spiritual covering.

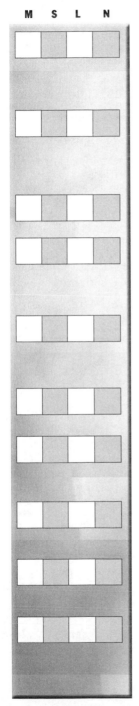

M S L N

27. I have an insatiable appetite for the presence of God.

28. Through God I have been used to reveal to others specific things that will happen in the future, and they have come to pass.

29. I have enjoyed assuming the responsibility for the spiritual well-being of a particular group of Christians.

30. I feel I can explain the New Testament teaching about the health and ministry of the Body of Christ in a relevant way.

31. I can intuitively arrive at solutions to fairly complicated problems.

32. I have had insights relating to spiritual truth that others have said helped bring them closer to God.

33. I can effectively motivate people to get busy and do what they are supposed to do.

34. I can "see" the Spirit of God resting on certain people from time to time.

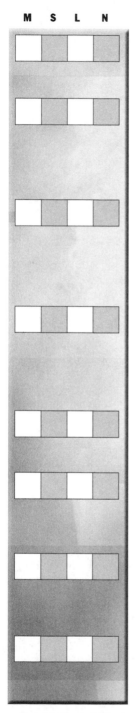

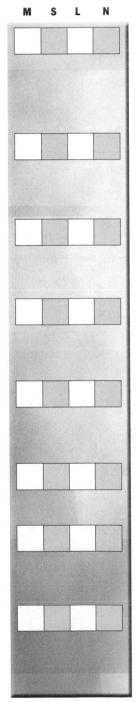

35. My giving records show that I contribute considerably more than 10 percent of my income to the Lord's work.

36. Other people have told me that I have helped them become more effective in their ministries.

37. I have offered to care for others when they have had material or physical needs.

38. I feel I could learn another language well in order to minister to those in a different culture.

39. I have shared joyfully how Christ has brought me to Himself in a way that is meaningful to nonbelievers.

40. I enjoy taking charge of church suppers or social events.

41. I have believed God for the impossible and seen it happen in a tangible way.

42. Other Christians have followed my leadership because they trusted me.

M S L N

43. I enjoy handling the details of organizing ideas, people, resources and time for more effective ministry.

44. God has used me personally to perform supernatural signs and wonders.

45. I enjoy praying for sick people because I know ahead of time that many of them will be healed as a result.

46. I have spoken an immediate message of God to His people in a language I have never learned.

47. I have interpreted public tongues with the result that the Body of Christ was edified, exhorted or comforted.

48. Living a simple lifestyle is an exciting challenge for me.

49. Other people have noted that I feel more indifferent about not being married than most.

50. When I hear an urgent prayer request, I pray for that need for several days at least.

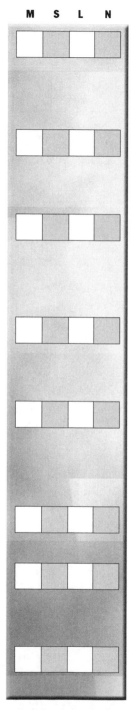

M S L N

51. I have actually heard a demon speak in a loud voice.

52. I don't have many special skills, but I volunteer to do what needs to be done around the church.

53. I am known as a leader of leaders.

54. I intuitively know what should happen next in a worship service.

55. People have told me that I have communicated timely and urgent messages that must have come directly from the Lord.

56. I feel unafraid of offering spiritual guidance and direction to a group of Christians.

57. I can devote considerable time to learning new biblical truths in order to communicate them to others.

58. When other people have a problem, I can frequently guide them to the best biblical solution.

59. Through study or experience I have discerned major strategies or techniques that God seems to use in furthering His kingdom.

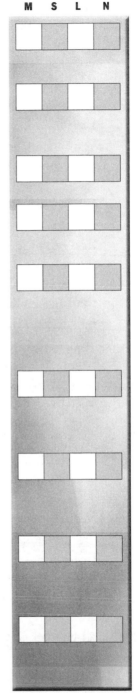

	M	S	L	N

60. People come to me in their afflictions or suffering because they know that I will listen to them and understand.

61. I can tell with a fairly high degree of assurance when a person is afflicted by an evil spirit.

62. When I am moved by an appeal to give to God's work, I usually can find the money I need to help.

63. I have enjoyed doing routine tasks that have allowed more effective ministry on the part of others.

64. I enjoy visiting in hospitals and/or retirement homes, and feel I do well in such a ministry.

65. People of a different race or culture have been attracted to me, and we have related well.

66. Non-Christians have noted that they feel comfortable when they are around me, and that I have a positive effect on them toward developing a faith in Christ.

67. When people come to our home, they indicate that they "feel at home" with us.

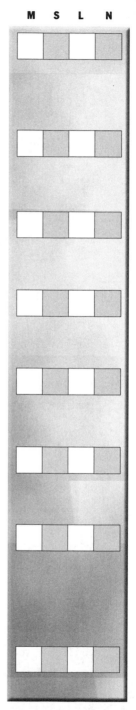

M   S   L   N

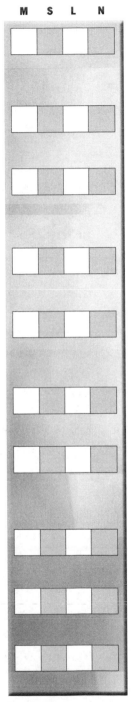

68. Other people have told me that I had faith to accomplish what seemed impossible to them.

69. When I set goals, others seem to accept them readily.

70. I have been able to make effective and efficient plans for accomplishing the goals of a group.

71. God regularly seems to do impossible things through my life.

72. Others have told me that God healed them of an emotional problem when I ministered to them.

73. I can speak to God in a language I have never learned.

74. I have prayed that I may interpret if someone begins speaking in tongues.

75. I am not poor, but I can warmly identify with poor people.

76. I am glad I have more time to serve the Lord because I am single.

77. Day in and day out, intercessory prayer is one of my favorite ways of spending time.

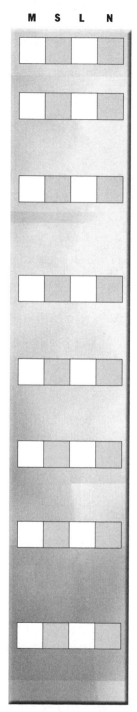

M S L N

78. Others call on me when they suspect that someone is demonized.

79. Others have mentioned that I seem to enjoy routine tasks and do well at them.

80. Christian leaders seem pleased to work under my leadership, and they respect my authority when we undertake a common task.

81. During worship, I can often tell if there is a spiritual force attempting to hinder our connection with God.

82. I sometimes have a strong sense of what God wants to say to people in response to particular situations.

83. I have helped fellow believers by guiding them to relevant portions of the Bible and praying with them.

84. I feel I can communicate significant truths to others and see resulting changes in knowledge, attitudes, values or conduct.

85. Some people indicate that I have perceived and applied biblical truths to the specific needs of fellow believers.

M   S   L   N

86. I study and read quite a bit in order to learn new biblical truths.

87. I have a desire to effectively counsel those in need.

88. I can recognize whether a person's teaching or actions are from God, from Satan, or of human origin.

89. I am so confident that God will meet my financial needs that I do not hesitate to give to His work sacrificially and consistently.

90. When I do things behind the scenes and others are helped, I am joyful.

91. People call on me to help those who are less fortunate.

92. I would be willing to leave comfortable surroundings if it would enable me to share Christ with less-fortunate people.

93. I get frustrated when others don't seem to share their faith with non-believers as much as I do.

94. Others have mentioned to me that I am a very hospitable person.

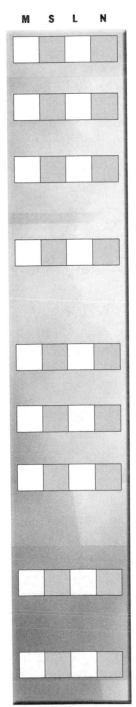

M S L N

95. There have been times when I have felt sure I knew God's specific will for the future growth of His work, even when others have not been so sure.

96. When I am part of a group, others seem to back off and expect me to take the leadership.

97. I am able to give directions to others without using persuasion to get them to accomplish a certain task.

98. People have told me that I was God's instrument that brought supernatural change in lives or circumstances.

99. I have prayed for others and instantaneous physical healing has often occurred.

100. When I give a public message in tongues, I expect it to be interpreted.

101. I have interpreted tongues in a way that seemed to bless others.

102. Others tell me that I sacrifice too much materially in order to fulfill God's calling.

M S L N

103. I am single and have little difficulty controlling my sexual desires.

104. Others have told me that my prayers for them have been answered in tangible ways.

105. Other people have been instantly delivered from demonic oppression when I have prayed.

106. I prefer being active and doing something rather than just sitting around talking or reading or listening to a speaker.

107. I regularly receive revelation from God as to what the Holy Spirit is currently saying to the Church.

108. Others have told me that my worship helps them enter into the presence of God.

109. I frequently feel that I know exactly what God wants to do in ministry at a specific point in time.

110. People with needs have told me that I have helped them be restored to the Christian community.

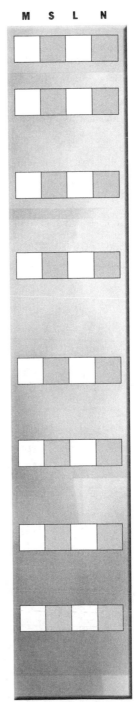

111. Studying the Bible and sharing my insights with others are very satisfying for me.

112. I have felt an unusual presence of God and personal confidence when important decisions needed to be made.

113. I have the ability to discover new truths for myself through reading or observing situations firsthand.

114. I have helped others find a biblical solution to their affliction or suffering.

115. I can tell whether a person speaking in tongues is genuine.

116. I have been willing to maintain a lower standard of living in order to benefit God's work.

117. When I serve the Lord, I truthfully don't care if someone else gets the credit for what I do.

118. I frequently enjoy spending time with a lonely, shut-in person or with someone in prison.

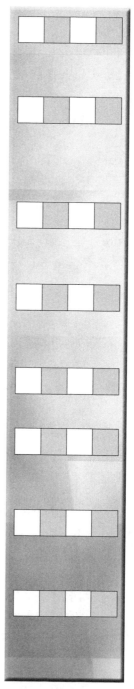

119. More than most, I have had a strong desire to see peoples of other countries won to the Lord.

120. I am attracted to nonbelievers mainly because of my desire to win them to Christ.

121. I have desired to make my home available to those in the Lord's service whenever needed.

122. Others have told me that I am a person of unusual vision, and I agree.

123. When I am in charge, things seem to run smoothly.

124. I have enjoyed bearing the responsibility for the success of a particular task within my church or in the workplace.

125. In the name of the Lord, I have been able to help blind people receive their sight.

126. When I pray for the sick, either I or they feel sensations of tingling or warmth.

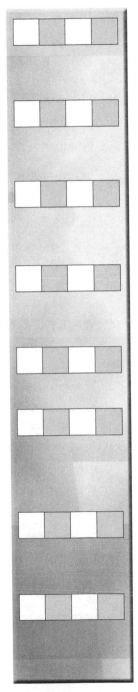

127. When I speak in tongues to a group, I believe it is edifying to the Lord's Body.

128. I have interpreted tongues in such a way that the message appeared to be directly from God.

129. Poor people accept me easily because I choose to live on their level.

130. I readily identify with Paul's desire for others to be single as he was.

131. When I pray, God frequently speaks to me, and I recognize His voice.

132. I regularly cast out demons in Jesus' name.

133. I respond cheerfully when asked to do a job, even if it seems menial.

134. When I call Christian leaders to come together for a certain purpose, a significant number of them respond.

135. I have a compelling desire to lead others into an experience with God.

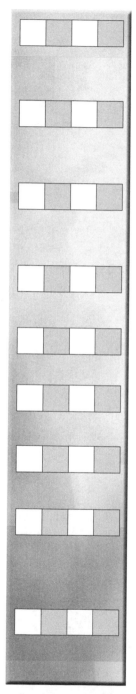

STEP 2: WAGNER-MODIFIED HOUTS CHART

In the grid below, enter the numerical value of each of your responses next to the number of the corresponding statement from *step 1*.

Much = 3   Some = 2   Little = 1   Not at All = 0

Then add up the five numbers that you have recorded in each row and place the sum in the "Total" column.

		Value of Answers				Total	Gift (see step 3)
A	1	28	55	82	109		Prophecy
B	2	29	56	83	110		Pastor
C	3	30	57	84	111		Teaching
D	4	31	58	85	112		Wisdom
E	5	32	59	86	113		Knowledge
F	6	33	60	87	114		Exhortation
G	7	34	61	88	115		Discerning of Spirits
H	8	35	62	89	116		Giving
I	9	36	63	90	117		Helps
J	10	37	64	91	118		Mercy
K	11	38	65	92	119		Missionary
L	12	39	66	93	120		Evangelist
M	13	40	67	94	121		Hospitality
N	14	41	68	95	122		Faith
O	15	42	69	96	123		Leadership
P	16	43	70	97	124		Administration
Q	17	44	71	98	125		Miracles
R	18	45	72	99	126		Healing
S	19	46	73	100	127		Tongues
T	20	47	74	101	128		Interpretation
U	21	48	75	102	129		Voluntary Poverty
V	22	49	76	103	130		Celibacy
W	23	50	77	104	131		Intercession
X	24	51	78	105	132		Deliverance
Y	25	52	79	106	133		Service
Z	26	53	80	107	134		Apostle
AA	27	54	81	108	135		Leading Worship

STEP 3: GIFT DEFINITIONS AND SCRIPTURE REFERENCES

The following pages contain *suggested* definitions of the 28 spiritual gifts covered in this book. Experience has shown that many people come with presuppositions about certain gifts, so in some cases a note of explanation has been added to the definition.

The questions on the Wagner-Modified Houts Questionnaire are premised on these definitions of the gifts.

A. **Prophecy:** The gift of prophecy is the special ability that God gives to certain members of the Body of Christ to receive and communicate an immediate message of God to His people through a divinely anointed utterance (see Luke 7:26; Acts 15:32; 21:9-11; Rom. 12:6; 1 Cor. 12:10,28; Eph. 4:11-13).

B. **Pastor:** The gift of pastor is the special ability that God gives to certain members of the Body of Christ to assume a long-term personal responsibility for the spiritual welfare of a group of believers (see John 10:1-18; Eph. 4:11-13; 1 Tim. 3:1-7; 1 Pet. 5:1-3). *Note:* The term "pastor" is commonly used to describe the leader of a local congregation; however, many who lead churches have dominant gifts other than pastor (e.g., leader or teacher). Those leaders who do not have the dominant gift of pastor may augment their role using volunteers or staff members.

C. **Teaching:** The gift of teaching is the special ability that God gives to certain members of the Body of Christ to communicate information relevant to the health and ministry of the Body and its members in such a way that others will learn (see Acts 18:24-28;

20:20-21; Rom. 12:7; 1 Cor. 12:28; Eph. 4:11-13).

D. **Wisdom:** The gift of wisdom is the special ability that God gives to certain members of the Body of Christ to know the mind of the Holy Spirit in such a way as to receive insight into how given knowledge may best be applied to specific needs arising in the Body of Christ (see Acts 6:3,10; 1 Cor. 2:1-13; 12:8; Jas. 1:5-6; 2 Pet. 3:15-16).

   Note: Pentecostals and charismatics often use the term "word of wisdom," meaning a revelatory message God gives to bring resolution to a certain situation. I feel the charismatic "word of wisdom" is really a subset of the gift of prophecy, not the gift of wisdom. A judge, on the other hand, would be one who has a gift of wisdom.

E. **Knowledge:** The gift of knowledge is the special ability that God gives to certain members of the Body of Christ to discover, accumulate, analyze and clarify information and ideas that are pertinent to the growth and well-being of the Body (see Acts 5:1-11; 1 Cor. 2:14; 12:8; 2 Cor. 11:6; Col. 2:2-3).

   Note: Pentecostals and charismatics often use the term "word of knowledge," which is information that God gives by revelation for a certain situation. My interpretation of the charismatic "word of knowledge" is that such a gift is in reality a subset of the gift of prophecy, not the gift of knowledge. A scholar, on the other hand, would be one who has a gift of knowledge.

F. **Exhortation:** The gift of exhortation—sometimes called the gift of counseling—is the special ability that God gives to certain members of the Body of

Christ to minister words of comfort, consolation, encouragement and counsel to other members of the Body in such a way that they feel helped and healed (see Acts 14:22; Rom. 12:8; 1 Tim. 4:13; Heb. 10:25).

G. **Discerning of Spirits:** The gift of discerning (or discernment) of spirits is the special ability that God gives to certain members of the Body of Christ to know with assurance whether certain behaviors purported to be of God are in reality divine, human or satanic (see Matt. 16:21-23; Acts 5:1-11; 16:16-18; 1 Cor. 12:10; 1 John 4:1-6).

H. **Giving:** The gift of giving is the special ability that God gives to certain members of the Body of Christ to contribute their material resources to the work of the Lord liberally and cheerfully, above and beyond the tithes and offerings expected of all believers (see Mark 12:41-44; Rom. 12:8; 2 Cor. 8:1-7; 9:2-8).

I. **Helps:** The gift of helps is the special ability that God gives to certain members of the Body of Christ to invest the talents they have in the life and ministry of other members of the Body, thus enabling those others to increase the effectiveness of their own spiritual gifts (see Mark 15:40-41; Luke 8:2-3; Acts 9:36; Rom. 16:1-2; 1 Cor. 12:28).
   Note: The gift of helps may be confused with the gift of service. Someone with the gift of helps usually aids one individual (e.g., an administrative assistant), while a person with the gift of service is willing to do whatever is necessary for a cause or project.

J. **Mercy:** The gift of mercy is the special ability that God gives to certain members of the Body of Christ to feel genuine empathy and compassion for individuals,

both Christian and non-Christian, who suffer distressing physical, mental or emotional problems, and
to translate that compassion into cheerfully done
deeds that reflect Christ's love and alleviate the suffering (see Matt. 20:29-34; 25:34-40; Mark 9:41; Luke
10:33-35; Acts 11:28-30; 16:33-34; Rom. 12:8).

K. **Missionary:** The gift of missionary is the special
ability that God gives to certain members of the
Body of Christ to minister whatever other spiritual
gifts they have in a second culture (see Acts 8:4; 13:2-
3; 22:21; Rom. 10:15; 1 Cor. 9:19-23; Eph. 3:6-8).
Note: The gift of missionary should not be confused
with the gift of apostle. Some apostles have the gift
of missionary and do cross-cultural ministry (e.g.,
the apostle Paul), while other apostles do not have
the missionary gift and therefore they minister
monoculturally (e.g., the apostle Peter).

L. **Evangelist:** The gift of evangelist is the special ability
that God gives to certain members of the Body of
Christ to share the gospel with unbelievers in such a
way that men and women become Jesus' disciples and
responsible members of the Body of Christ (see Acts
8:5-6,26-40; 14:21; 21:8; Eph. 4:11-13; 2 Tim. 4:5).

M. **Hospitality:** The gift of hospitality is the special ability that God gives to certain members of the Body of
Christ to provide an open house and warm welcome
for those in need of food and lodging (see Acts 16:14-
15; Rom. 12:9-13; 16:23; Heb. 13:1-2; 1 Pet. 4:9).

N. **Faith:** The gift of faith is the special ability that God
gives to certain members of the Body of Christ to discern with extraordinary confidence the will and purposes of God for the future of His work (see Acts

11:22-24; 27:21-25; Rom. 4:18-21; 1 Cor. 12:9; Heb. 11).

O. **Leadership:** The gift of leadership is the special ability that God gives to certain members of the Body of Christ to set goals in accordance with God's purpose for the future and to communicate these goals to others in such a way that they voluntarily and harmoniously work together to accomplish those goals for the glory of God (see Luke 9:51; Acts 7:10; 15:7-11; Rom. 12:8; 1 Tim. 5:17; Heb. 13:17).

P. **Administration:** The gift of administration is the special ability that God gives to certain members of the Body of Christ to understand clearly the immediate and long-range goals of a particular unit of the Body and to devise and execute effective plans for the accomplishment of those goals (see Luke 14:28-30; Acts 6:1-7; 27:11; 1 Cor. 12:28; Titus 1:5).

Q. **Miracles:** The gift of miracles is the special ability that God gives to certain members of the Body of Christ to serve as human intermediaries through whom it pleases God to perform powerful acts that are perceived by observers to have altered the ordinary course of nature (see Acts 9:36-42; 19:11-20; 20:7-12; Rom. 15:18-19; 1 Cor. 12:10,28; 2 Cor. 12:12).

R. **Healing:** The gift of healing is the special ability that God gives to certain members of the Body of Christ to serve as human intermediaries through whom it pleases God to cure illness and restore health apart from the use of natural means (see Acts 3:1-10; 5:12-16; 9:32-35; 28:7-10; 1 Cor. 12:9,28).

S. **Tongues:** The gift of tongues is the special ability that God gives to certain members of the Body of Christ (1) to speak to God in a language they have never learned and/or (2) to receive and communicate an immediate message from God to His people through a divinely anointed utterance in a language they have never learned (see Mark 16:17; Acts 2:1-13; 10:44-46; 19:1-7; 1 Cor. 12:10,28; 14:13-19).

T. **Interpretation of Tongues:** The gift of interpretation of tongues is the special ability that God gives to certain members of the Body of Christ to make known in the vernacular the message of one who speaks in tongues (see 1 Cor. 12:10,30; 14:13-14,26-28).

U. **Voluntary Poverty:** The gift of voluntary poverty is the special ability that God gives to certain members of the Body of Christ to serve God more effectively by renouncing material comfort and luxury and to adopt a personal lifestyle equivalent to those living at the poverty level in a given society in order to serve God more effectively (see Acts 2:44-45; 4:34-37; 1 Cor. 13:1-3; 2 Cor. 6:10; 8:9).

V. **Celibacy:** The gift of celibacy is the special ability that God gives to certain members of the Body of Christ to remain single and enjoy it and not suffer undue sexual temptations (see Matt. 19:10-12; 1 Cor. 7:7-8).

W. **Intercession:** The gift of intercession is the special ability that God gives to certain members of the Body of Christ to pray for extended periods of time on a regular basis and see frequent and specific answers to their prayers to a degree much greater than that which is expected of the average Christian (see Luke 22:41-44; Acts 12:12; Col. 1:9-12; 4:12-13; 1 Tim. 2:1-2; Jas. 5:14-16).

X. **Deliverance:** The gift of deliverance is the special ability that God gives to certain members of the Body of Christ to cast out demons and evil spirits (see Matt. 12:22-32; Luke 10:12-20; Acts 8:5-8; 16:16-18).

Note: This gift has also been referred to as the gift of exorcism; however, that term has been degraded by its frequent use by those practicing occult exorcism, a counterfeit form of deliverance.

Y. **Service:** The gift of service—sometimes called the gift of volunteer—is the special ability that God gives to certain members of the Body of Christ to identify the unmet needs involved in a task related to God's work, and to make use of available resources to meet those needs and help accomplish the desired goals (see Acts 6:1-7; Rom. 12:7; Gal. 6:2,10; 2 Tim. 1:16-18; Titus 3:14).

Note: The gift of service may be confused with the gift of helps. See note on helps for clarification.

Z. **Apostle:** The gift of apostle is the special ability that God gives to certain members of the Body of Christ to assume and to exercise divinely imparted authority in order to establish the foundational government of an assigned sphere of ministry within the Church. An apostle hears from the Holy Spirit and sets things in order accordingly for the Church's health, growth, maturity and outreach (see Luke 6:12-13; 1 Cor. 12:28; Eph. 2:20; 4:11-13).

Note: "Church" refers to the believers who gather weekly and also to the believers scattered in the workplace.

AA. **Leading Worship:** The gift of leading worship is the special ability that God gives to certain members of the Body of Christ to accurately discern the heart of God for a particular public worship service, to draw others into an intimate experience of God during the worship time and to allow the Holy Spirit to change directions and emphases as the service progresses (see 1 Sam. 16:23; 1 Chron. 9:33; 2 Chron. 5:12-14; Ps. 34:3).

STEP 4: GIFTS AND MINISTRIES ANALYSIS

1. Using the results of the scoring chart in *step 2*, enter below in the "Dominant" section your three highest-rated gifts. Then enter in the "Subordinate" section the next three highest-scoring gifts. In case of some ties, do not hesitate to add lines to the "Dominant" section. This will give you a *tentative* evaluation of where your gifts may lie.

   Dominant: 1. _____

                 2. _____

                 3. _____

   Subordinate: 1. _____

                 2. _____

                 3. _____

2. What ministries are you *now* performing (formally or informally) in the Body?

   _____

   _____

   _____

   _____

   _____

   _____

   _____

   _____

   _____

3. Are there any of these ministries that you are not especially gifted for? If so, God may be calling you to consider changes.

_____

_____

_____

_____

_____

_____

_____

_____

_____

4. Is your vocational status lay or clergy?

_____

5. In light of your gift cluster and vocational status, what are some ministry models or roles suitable for you? What specific roles in the Body of Christ, including the workplace, has God possibly gifted you for?

_____

_____

_____

_____

_____

_____

_____

_____

_____

6. Discuss your findings with other believers who know you in order to evaluate your conclusions. Record their comments in the space provided.

SCRIPTURE INDEX

SUBJECT INDEX

diakonion, 76
diakonos, 212
discerning of spirits, gift of, 99-101
Discover Your Spiritual Gift and Use It, 180, 181
discovering spiritual gifts, 36-40, 109-133, 236, 239-242
domata, 34
Duquesne Weekend, 11
Dynamics of Spiritual Gifts, The, 81

Edge, Findley B., 123-124
Eighth Day of Creation, 50, 81, 134
ekklesia, 35
Embassy of the Blessed Kingdom of God for All Nations, 209-210
energematon, 76
Engstrom, Ted, 131
Era of the Spirit, The, 81
Erickson, Paul, 42
evangelism, 235
    and deliverance, 103-104
    cross-cultural, 185-189
    definition of, 166-167
    E-0, 184-185
    E-1, 184-187
    E-2, 184-191
    E-3, 184-191
    emphasis of, 169-171
    persuasion, 167
    presence, 166
    proclamation, 167
Evangelism Explosion, 72, 173
evangelist
    gift of, 54, 62, 76, 120, 125, 162-180, 191
    office of, 15
    varieties of, 165-166
exhortation, gift of, 53, 149-151
exorcism versus deliverance, 108
experience, spiritual, 22

faith, 87, 112, 242-243
    gift of, 54, 87, 153-157
    measure of, 25, 27, 35, 76
feelings, personal, 121-124, 129
Fellowship Bible Church, 38
Finding Your Spiritual Gifts, 121
Fire in the Fireplace, 18
First Baptist Church of Modesto, 238
First Covenant Church, 42
First Evangelical Free Church, 106, 159
Flynn, Leslie B., 77, 80, 150
Ford, Leighton, 164-165, 177, 207
Four Spiritual Laws, 173, 176
fruit of the Spirit, 82, 84-86
Fuller, Charles E., 166
Fuller Seminary, 7, 118, 177

Gangel, Kenneth O., 225
Gasson, Raphael, 97-98
Gee, Donald, 77, 217, 223
George Muller: The Man of Faith, 50, 107
Getz, Gene A., 37-40
gift
    of administration, 54, 130-131, 151-153
    of apostle, 6-7, 54, 192-200
    of celibacy, 57-61, 88
    of deliverance, 7, 69, 101-104, 226
    of discerning of spirits, 99-101
    of evangelist, 54, 62, 76, 120, 125, 162-180, 191
    of exhortation, 53, 149-151
    of faith, 54, 87, 153-157
    of giving, 53, 90-93, 96
    of healing, 15, 54, 223-224, 225-228
    of helps, 54, 208, 210-211
    of hospitality, 57, 65-69, 87
    of intercession, 62, 69-73
    of interpretation of tongues, 54, 212-214, 222-223
    of knowledge, 54, 203-206, 216-217
    of leadership, 53, 152, 157-159
    of leading worship, 7, 69, 73-75
    of martyrdom, 7, 57, 62, 65
    of mercy, 53, 208-210
    of miracles, 15, 54, 223-225
    of missionary, 57, 62, 182-201, 205-206
    of pastor, 54, 75-76, 124, 135-160
    of prophecy, 6, 53, 212-218
    of service, 53, 208, 211-212
    of teaching, 53, 75-76, 84, 126-129, 204-205
    of tongues, 15, 54, 212-214, 218-221
    of voluntary poverty, 57, 62, 93-96
    of wisdom, 53, 203, 206-208
gift confusion, 191-192
gift exaltation, 45-46
Gift Is Not Mine, The, 229
gift-mix, 31, 60, 138, 142-143, 204-206
    in churches, 77-79, 114, 233-234
gift projection, 46-49, 60, 67-68, 92, 95, 155-157, 172-178, 190-191, 221
gift theology, 25-27, 47
Gifts of the Spirit, The, 50, 134, 161, 229
Gillquist, Peter, 235
giving, gift of, 53, 90-93, 96
Global Harvest Ministries, 102

Now Christians Can Easily Find and Use Their God-Given Spiritual Gifts

Your Spiritual Gifts Can Help Your Church Grow
The Best-Selling Guide for Discovering and Understanding Your Unique Spiritual Gifts and Using them to Bless Others
C. Peter Wagner
ISBN 08307.36972

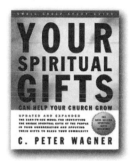

Your Spiritual Gifts Can Help Your Church Grow Small Group Study Guide
The Easy-to-Use Model for Identifying the Unique Spiritual Gifts of the People in Your Congregation and Applying Their Gifts to Bless Your Community
C. Peter Wagner
ISBN 08307.36646

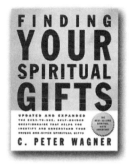

Finding Your Spiritual Gifts
The Easy-to-Use, Self-Guided Questionnaire That Helps You Identify and Understand Your Unique God-Given Spiritual Gifts
C. Peter Wagner
ISBN 08307.36948

Discover Your Spiritual Gifts
The Easy-to-Use Guide That Helps You Identify and Understand Your Unique God-Given Spiritual Gifts
C. Peter Wagner
ISBN 08307.36786

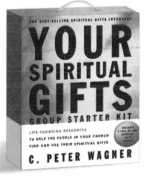

Your Spiritual Gifts Group Starter Kit
Life-Changing Resources to Help the People In Your Church Find and Use Their Spiritual Gifts
C. Peter Wagner
ISBN 08307.36824